Google+

the missing manual®

The book that should have come with the site

Kevin Purdy

O'REILLY®

Beijing | Cambridge | Farnham | Köln | Sebastopol | Tokyo

Google+: The Missing Manual
By Kevin Purdy

Published by O'Reilly Media, Inc., 1005 Gravenstein Highway North, Sebastopol, CA 95472.

O'Reilly books may be purchased for educational, business, or sales promotional use. Online editions are also available for most titles (*safari.oreilly.com*). For more information, contact our corporate/institutional sales department: 800.998.9938 or *corporate@oreilly.com*.

Editor: Dawn Mann	**Cover Designers:** Monica Kamsvaag and
Production Editor: Jasmine Perez	Randy Comer
Proofreader: Nan Reinhardt	**Interior Designers:** Ron Bilodeau and
Illustrations: Rob Romano	J.D. Biersdorfer
Indexer: Ron Strauss	

December 2011:   First Edition.

Revision History for the 1st Edition:

2011-12-07   First release

See *http://oreilly.com/catalog/errata.csp?isbn=9781449311872* for release details.

ISBN: 978-1-449-31187-2
[LSI]

Contents

CHAPTER 4

Notifications. **73**
Where You Get Notifications 74
Controlling Which Notifications You Receive. 85
Making Notifications Less Intrusive 90

CHAPTER 5

Sharing Photos and Videos **93**
Viewing Photos 94
Sharing Photos. 98
Getting Photos onto Google+. 100
Tagging Photos 113
Editing and Deleting Photos. 116
Adjusting Overall Photo Settings. 123
Sharing Videos. 125

CHAPTER 6

Hanging Out **129**
Starting a Hangout 130
Hanging Out 136
Hangouts on Mobile Devices. 146
Tips for Better Hangouts 147

CHAPTER 7

Searching and Sparks **151**
Searching Google+ 152
Getting Better Results. 158
Saving Searches 161
Throw Your Post into the Mix with Hashtags 164

CHAPTER 8

Google+ Mobile **169**
Getting Google+ onto Your Phone. 170
Streams, Posts, and Circles. 174
Viewing Photos 181
Starting a Messenger Session (Apps Only) 183
Mobile Notifications 187
Posting to Google+ via Text Message. 188
Sending Things to Google+ from Other Apps (Android Only) 189

The Missing Credits

About the Author

Kevin Purdy is a guy from upstate New York who some-how convinced the founding editor of software and productivity blog Lifehacker to take a chance on a young newspaper reporter with a secret geek life. He blogged at Lifehacker for over three years, and somehow managed to write *The Complete Android Guide* during that time. He now makes a living writing for whoever will have his words, and doesn't make much of a living organizing TEDxBuffalo, obsessing over homemade specialty coffee, and hosting the In Pod Form podcast. He lives in Buffalo, NY, with his wife and two cats. Email: *kspurdy@gmail.com*.

About the Creative Team

Dawn Mann (editor) is associate editor for the Missing Manual series. When not reading about Google+, she beads, bikes, and causes trouble. Email: *dawn@oreilly.com*.

Jasmine Perez (production editor) spends her free time cooking vegetarian meals, listening to her favorite freeform radio station, WFMU, and going on adventures whenever possible. Email: *jperez@oreilly.com*.

Cassandra Moffitt (technical reviewer) is the lead graphic designer at Going to the Sun Marketing (*www.gttsmarketing.com*), a full-service marketing agency with offices in New York and Montana. She enjoys car racing and all things tech and gaming.

Nan Reinhardt (proofreader) is a freelance copyeditor and proofreader, who is also a writer of romantic fiction. Her debut novel is due out in February 2012 and she has two novels with her agent at Curtis Brown Literary Agency. In between editing gigs, she is busy working on her fourth book. She blogs thrice weekly at *www.nanreinhardt.com*. Email: *reinhardt8@comcast.net*.

Ron Strauss (indexer) lives with his wife in northern California at 2,300 feet. When not indexing Missing Manuals, he moonlights as a musician (viola and Native American flute).

Acknowledgments

Editor Dawn Mann is a rock, and she knows how to roll with both a fast-moving subject and an occasionally sideways-running author. Cassandra Moffitt has the sharpest eyes around when it comes to catching buttons, clicks, and overly clever site designs. Web-syncing software Dropbox kept the book's chapters and images safe and accessible at all times, and Snagit made all these screenshots possible. The support, and how-to training, provided by Gina Trapani and Adam Pash were invaluable. And none of this would be possible without my wife, to whom I owe quite a few home-cooked meals.

The Missing Manual Series

Missing Manuals are witty, superbly written guides to computer products that don't come with printed manuals (which is just about all of them). Each book features a handcrafted index and cross-references to specific pages (not just chapters).

Recent and upcoming titles:

Access 2010: The Missing Manual by Mathew MacDonald

Buying a Home: The Missing Manual by Nancy Conner

Best iPhone Apps, 2nd Edition by J.D. Biersdorfer

CSS: The Missing Manual, Second Edition, by David Sawyer McFarland

Creating a Website: The Missing Manual, Second Edition, by Matthew MacDonald

David Pogue's Digital Photography: The Missing Manual by David Pogue

Dreamweaver CS5: The Missing Manual by David Sawyer McFarland

Excel 2010: The Missing Manual by Matthew MacDonald

Facebook: The Missing Manual, Second Edition by E.A. Vander Veer

FileMaker Pro 11: The Missing Manual by Susan Prosser and Stuart Gripman

Flash CS5: The Missing Manual by Chris Grover

iMovie '09 & iDVD: The Missing Manual by David Pogue and Aaron Miller

iPad: The Missing Manual by J.D. Biersdorfer

iPhone: The Missing Manual, 4th Edition by David Pogue

iPhone App Development: The Missing Manual by Craig Hockenberry

iPhoto '09: The Missing Manual by David Pogue and J.D. Biersdorfer

JavaScript: The Missing Manual by David Sawyer McFarland

Living Green: The Missing Manual by Nancy Conner

Mac OS X: The Missing Manual, Leopard Edition by David Pogue

Mac OS X Snow Leopard: The Missing Manual by David Pogue

Microsoft Project 2010: The Missing Manual by Bonnie Biafore

Netbooks: The Missing Manual by J.D. Biersdorfer

Office 2010: The Missing Manual by Nancy Connor, Chris Grover, and Matthew MacDonald

Personal Investing: The Missing Manual by Bonnie Biafore

Photoshop CS5: The Missing Manual by Lesa Snider

Photoshop Elements 9: The Missing Manual by Barbara Brundage

QuickBase: The Missing Manual by Nancy Conner

QuickBooks 2011: The Missing Manual by Bonnie Biafore

Quicken 2009: The Missing Manual by Bonnie Biafore

Switching to the Mac: The Missing Manual, Leopard Edition by David Pogue

Switching to the Mac: The Missing Manual, Snow Leopard Edition by David Pogue

Windows 7: The Missing Manual by David Pogue

Your Body: The Missing Manual by Matthew MacDonald

Your Brain: The Missing Manual by Matthew MacDonald

Your Money: The Missing Manual by J.D. Roth

Introduction

DESPITE WHAT YOU MIGHT think based on its name, Google+ isn't a super-charged version of the search engine we all turn to for answers. And it's not a paid upgrade for businesses, or an exclusive club for people who are really, really good at searching Google. Nope, it's actually a big, daring move by a company primarily known for search, advertising, and making millionaires out of computer geeks into the relatively new field of *social networking*—websites, like Facebook and Twitter, that let you link up with friends, acquaintances, and maybe even celebrities and brands you like.

Since its launch as an invite-only site in June 2011, Google+ has picked up an estimated 40 million users, and it's being integrated into more and more of Google's other services, like Gmail and Google Docs. So Google+ is more than just a way to connect with friends, family, and acquaintances online. It's a smarter way of sharing online that's tied into all the other Google services you might already use. And this book explains how to get the most out of Google+, whether you're using it for fun or business, on a Windows computer, a Mac, an Android phone, iPhone, or just about anywhere you can get on the Web (or even just send a text message).

How Google+ Works

DESPITE WHAT YOU MIGHT have read about it in the press, Google+ isn't quite Google's version of Facebook. Google+ does let you do some of the same things you can do on Facebook—and Twitter, and even LinkedIn. You can use Google+ to find people you know, people you used to know, friends-of-friends with whom you share common interests, and even—if you'd like—complete strangers. It's especially easy to build that network of connections if you've been using other Google tools like Gmail, the web-based email program, but it's not hard for complete newcomers to the Google-verse to use, either. Once you create a network of people on Google+, however big or small, you can share all kinds of things with those friends and acquaintances: thoughts and updates, photos, videos, links to interesting websites, your location, and even a round of poker or some other game.

But Facebook (and in some cases, Twitter) offers most of those same features, so how is Google+ different? For one thing, it adds some neat, unique offerings. *hangouts* are the best example—they let you hold group video chats with up to 10 people (see Chapter 6). There's also *Messenger*, which can help you keep a group conversation going when people are out in the field; it's far more efficient than text-messaging and emailing (see page 183). And the photos, videos, and notifications about new stuff are a lot less cluttered, less intrusive, and easier to customize than on other social-networking sites.

What Google+ *really* does differently, though, is give you nearly total control over who can see each thing you put on Google+, and what kinds of things you see and from whom. For example, if you have an update about a local issue, like your favorite restaurant closing down, you can share that with just the folks who live nearby, and spare the people you know through your photography class from seeing that nice-but-irrelevant-to-them post. You arrange people into groups like Baby Picture Addicts, and browse their offerings only when you're in the mood for first steps, footie pajamas, and so on. And you have more control over how and when your life and thoughts get shared in Google+: who can tag you in photos, how far people can share your posts, who can bug you about games they're playing, and more.

All you need to get started with Google+ is an email address and a Google account (they're both free). You already have a Google account if you use any of Google's online services—Gmail, Google Docs, Picasa Web Albums, and so on— but it's easy to sign up for one if you don't (page 2 tells you how). And if your company or organization uses Google to host their email and other web tools, you can sign up for Google+ using that email address instead.

What You Can Do on Google+

AFTER YOU SIGN UP and sign in, you'll drop right into Google+, where you'll discover the different aspects of the site (all of which are explained in detail throughout this book):

- **Profile.** Where you control exactly what the general public, specific groups of people, or even just individuals (like your boss or mother-in-law) can see about you.

- **Circles.** The places where you'll organize the folks you know into groups so it's easy to share stuff with just the right people.

- **Streams.** The main page of Google+, where you see all the updates, pictures, news, and notes from people you know, and where you post your own contributions.

- **Photos.** Google+ makes it really easy to view photos, and to upload and share them with both your Google+ contacts and people who aren't (yet) members.

- **Notifications.** Google+ can let you know when there's a new photo of you, a comment on a post you wrote, or something else relevant to you happens. These notices can take several forms: emails, text messages sent to your cellphone, or notes displayed in a handy toolbar button on any Google site. Fortunately, it's easy to control what kinds of things Google+ tells you about (and how) so you don't get overwhelmed.

- **Hangouts.** The video chat service that's really easy and smooth to use, whether it's just you and one other person, or a whole football squad's worth of chatters.

- **Search.** Find people you know on Google+, see what your friends and others are saying about any subject, and keep on top of the latest news about a topic by seeing the news items that people on Google+ are linking to.

- **Mobile.** Google+ on an iPhone, Android phone, or in a mobile browser is a great way to show folks where you are, what you're doing, and share pictures of your adventures. There's also a built-in tool for managing groups of people while you're all on the go.

- **Games.** The fun part, where you solve puzzles, populate crime families, and fling *Angry Birds* at egg-stealing pigs.

NOTE This book covers the ins and outs of Google+ as they were when this book was being written. But since the site is changing so quickly, it's possible you may run into a feature that works different than described here, or a new feature that isn't covered in this book. If that happens, check out Google's help pages, which are actually quite helpful. To view them, click the gear icon in the upper-right corner of any Google+ page and select "Google+ help." You can use the search box that appears in the upper-right of the page to get info about whatever's vexing you.

About This Book

YOU MIGHT HAVE ALREADY heard that Google+ gives you better control over your social networking, but what does that mean, exactly? And where does Google+ fit into your life if you're already using Facebook, and maybe Twitter, too? And how can you use Google+ on your cellphone, tablet, or other web-friendly device?

This book explains all those things and more. You'll get a smooth introduction to Google+, one that won't leave you looking like you've just learned how to use your mouse. You'll learn what you can do with the site—and how to do it better. This book explores and explains the much-touted features of Google+, and covers details and perks that make the site so appealing to fiddlers (like your humble author). And you'll get a firm sense of how your public profile is used on Google+ and learn ways to protect your privacy.

This book is aimed at people of all skill levels. Don't have a Google account? No problem—this book walks you through getting one, and explains how Google+ connects with other Google services you might like. Already rocking out on the Web, but want to understand how Google+ fits into your web existence? This book makes the case for using the site and gives you the know-how to use it well, but also outlines its limitations.

> **NOTE** Most of the screenshots in this book were taken on a Windows computer running Chrome, the free web browser from Google. (You can learn more about Chrome at *www.google.com/chrome*.) And unless otherwise specified, most of the images of cellphone screens were taken on a phone running Android (*http://tinyurl.com/gpdroid*), version 2.3 (a.k.a. Gingerbread), also from Google. So if you use a Mac, a different browser, or a different type of phone, don't be alarmed if what you see on your screen doesn't exactly match the images you see in the following pages. You should still be able to follow the instructions in this book; any major differences between, say, Android and iPhone are noted in the text.

The Very Basics

TO USE THIS BOOK (and Google+), you need to know a few basics. This book assumes that you're familiar with a few terms and concepts:

- **Clicking.** This book includes instructions that require you to use your computer's mouse or trackpad. To *click* means to point your cursor (the arrow pointer) at something on the screen and then—without moving the cursor at all—press and release the left button on the mouse (or laptop trackpad). To *right-click* means the same thing, but pressing the *right* mouse button instead. (Usually, clicking selects an onscreen element or presses an onscreen button, whereas right-clicking typically reveals a *shortcut menu*, which lists some common tasks specific to whatever you're right-clicking.) To *double-click*, of course, means to click twice in rapid succession, again without moving the pointer at all. And to *drag* means to move the cursor while holding down the (left) mouse button the entire time.

  When you're told to *Shift-click* something, you click while pressing the Shift key. Related procedures, like *Ctrl-clicking*, work the same way—just click while pressing the corresponding key.

- **Keyboard shortcuts.** Nothing is faster than keeping your fingers on your keyboard to enter data, choose names, trigger commands, and so on—without losing time by grabbing the mouse, carefully positioning it, and then choosing a command or list entry. That's why many experienced Google fans prefer to trigger commands by pressing combinations of keys on the keyboard. For example, in most word processors, you can press Ctrl+B to produce a boldface word. In this book, when you read an instruction like "Press Ctrl+C to copy the text," start by pressing the Ctrl key; while it's down, type the letter C; and then release both keys.

About the Online Resources

AS THE OWNER OF a Missing Manual, you've got more than just a book to read. Online, you'll find example files so you can get some hands-on experience, as well as tips, articles, and maybe even a video or two. You can also communicate with the Missing Manual team and tell us what you love (or hate) about the book. Head over to *www.missingmanuals.com*, or go directly to one of the following sections.

Missing CD

This book doesn't have a CD pasted inside the back cover, but you're not missing out on anything. Go to *www.missingmanuals.com/cds*, where you'll find a list of clickable links to all the websites in this book so you don't wear down your fingers typing long web addresses.

Registration

If you register this book at oreilly.com, you'll be eligible for special offers—like discounts on future editions of *Google+: The Missing Manual.* Registering takes only a few clicks. To get started, type *www.oreilly.com/register* into your browser to hop directly to the Registration page.

Feedback

Got questions? Need more information? Fancy yourself a book reviewer? On our Feedback page, you can get expert answers to questions that come to you while reading, share your thoughts on this Missing Manual, and find groups for folks who share your interest in Google+. To have your say, go to *www.missing manuals.com/feedback*.

Errata

In an effort to keep this book as up to date and accurate as possible, each time we print more copies, we'll make any confirmed corrections you've suggested. We also note such changes on the book's website, so you can mark important corrections into your own copy of the book, if you like. Go to *http://tinyurl.com/gpluserrata* to report an error and view existing corrections.

Safari® Books Online

SAFARI® BOOKS ONLINE IS an on-demand digital library that lets you easily search over 7,500 technology and creative reference books and videos to find the answers you need quickly.

With a subscription, you can read any page and watch any video from our library online. Read books on your cellphone and mobile devices. Access new titles before they're available for print, get exclusive access to manuscripts in development, and post feedback for the authors. Copy and paste code samples, organize your favorites, download chapters, bookmark key sections, create notes, print out pages, and benefit from tons of other time-saving features.

O'Reilly Media has uploaded this book to the Safari Books Online service. To have full digital access to this book and others on similar topics from O'Reilly and other publishers, sign up for free at *http://my.safaribooksonline.com*.

CHAPTER 1

Getting Started

ONLINE SOCIAL NETWORKING IS A YOUNG BUT CROWDED FIELD, and any new site that makes people jump through hoops to get started isn't long for this world. Luckily, getting started with Google+ is easy, and if you already use another one of Google's services, diving in might require just a click or two.

Once you sign in, you get to decide how you want to use Google+. You can use it to connect with a very select group of friends, or to network with acquaintances, friends-of-friends, and the wider public through your profile and posts. The best part is that you get the final say over who can see every little bit of info you put online.

This chapter walks you through setting up your account, creating your profile, and setting visibility options to control who gets to see what.

Signing In and Joining Up

AS IS THE CASE with most Google offerings (such as Gmail, Google Docs, and Google Calendar), you need a Google account to use Google+. Most people get a Google account by signing up for Gmail, Google's free email service (if you use Gmail, hop to the next paragraph), but you don't need a Gmail address to use Google+. As long as you have *some* kind of email address, you can sign up for a Google account by heading to *www.google.com/accounts*. Simply click the "Sign up for a new Google Account" link in the upper right of that page, fill in the fields that appear, and then click "I accept. Create my account."

As of this writing, Google+ is in *beta*, which means that some features might not work properly and some features may change abruptly. One aspect of Google+ that has changed since the site first launched is that you're no longer *required* to have an invitation from somebody already set up with a Google+ account. Here are your options:

- **If you have an invitation email,** the process is slightly different depending on whether you use Gmail. Whatever kind of email address you have, click the red "Join Google+" button in the invitation email. Here's what happens next:

  - **If you use Gmail** you'll see the box shown here, which already has your first name and last name filled in.

○ **If you have an email address for your company or organization's Google Apps setup** (in other words, you sign into a site like *www.google.com/a/ something.com* to get to your email), you can sign in with that account—just enter your full *name@something.com* email address in the email field.

○ **If you use an email provider other than Gmail,** you'll see the Join Google+ screen. Click the red Sign In button to display the "Sign in with your Google Account" screen. Enter the full email address you used to create your Google account and your password, and then click the "Sign in" button. This takes you to the screen shown here.

NOTE If you like, you can invite others to join Google+. The box on page 4 explains how.

• **If you don't have an invitation,** simply head to *www.plus.google.com*. Click the red Sign In button and, on the page that appears, enter the full email address you used to create your Google account and your password, and then click the "Sign in" button. This takes you to the screen shown here.

TIP If typing web addresses by hand that isn't your idea of a good time, go to this book's Missing CD page at *www.missingmanuals.com/cds* (yes, you'll have to type that one by hand—sorry), where you'll find a clickable list of all the web addresses mentioned in this book.

Inviting Friends

Even though you don't need an invitation to join Google+, sending invitations to friends who aren't yet members can help them get started more quickly, and gives you more people to interact with. To send an invite, log into Google+ and then click the Google+ logo at the top of the screen to make sure you're on your Home page. On the right side of that page, click the "Invite friends" button. (If you don't see this button, don't panic: It's likely to disappear in the near future, since having an invitation is no longer a requirement for joining Google+.)

The dialog box that appears gives you a couple of options: You can invite friends individually by clicking the "+ Add people to invite" field and either typing out the name of someone who's in your Gmail, Yahoo, Hotmail, or other address book, or typing in a few friends' email addresses (separated by commas); either way, click "Send email" when you're done. A more efficient method is to select the link in the lower box, copy it by pressing Ctrl+C (⌘-C on a Mac), and then heading over to a different a social networking site you use—Facebook, Twitter, LinkedIn, or the like—and pasting it into a status update by pressing Ctrl+V (⌘-V on a Mac). That way, anyone who wants to join Google+ can do so by clicking the link in your post.

Invite people to join you on Google+

Invite people by email.

> + Add people to invite   `Send email`

Or, share this link with a group of people

The first step in using Google + is to create a Google *profile*, a page that shows just a bit about you or a whole lot, depending on your preference. How much you share, and with whom, is up to you. The box that reads "To join, create a public Google profile" only asks for your first name, last name, and gender (Male, Female, or Other), and possibly your birthday. All of these fields are required. You'll learn how to flesh out your profile starting on page 9.

Google+ has a fairly strict "common name" policy, at least as of this writing. That means they don't want you to sign up under a pseudonym, brand name, parody name (God, Fake Steve Jobs), or anything other than your real name. Google isn't reaching through your keyboard and fingerprinting you, but if their moderators or automatic search tools discover that you're using a fake name, you'll be asked to change it, and you could be booted off Google+ if you don't comply. Once you've signed up under your real name, however, you can then set up a *Page* for a company, brand, or even a fictitious entity—see this book's Missing CD page for details (*www.missingmanuals.com/cds*).

Google+ also suggests uploading a photo to "Help your friends recognize you." While you don't *have* to add a photo, it's a good idea because it lets people know they've found you and not someone else who shares your name. That way, you'll spare your friends from awkward "Do I know you?" conversations with strangers. If you're a Google enthusiast or veteran of Google Buzz (a predecessor of Google+ that wasn't very well received), you might already see an image on this first sign-up page. If not, or if you'd like to use a different photo, click the "Add photo" link or the silhouette next to it, and you'll be prompted to pick a photo.

If you're on your own computer and have a few pictures of yourself that you like, click the "Select a photo from your computer" button. In the file-selection box that appears, find the image you want to use (it can be a JPEG, GIF, or PNG file) and double-click it. Don't worry if it's not cropped properly, or even if it could look a bit better—you'll be able to make those edits right in Google+, without needing any other software, as explained in a moment.

> **TIP** If you use Firefox, Chrome, Safari, or certain other browsers besides Internet Explorer, the "Select profile photo" dialog box gives you the option of selecting a photo by dragging instead. The process is just like moving a file on your computer with the mouse: Line up your web browser so you can see the image file you want (whether it's saved on your desktop or you've located it in a file-viewing program like Windows Explorer, for example) and then simply drag the file into the dotted-line box within the "Select profile photo" dialog box. (If you use IE, you won't see this dotted-line box.)

If you use Google's Picasa Web Albums to store photos, you can click "Your photos" on the left-hand side of the "Select profile photo" dialog box and then pick a photo from your gallery. The other, less convenient options listed there are "Photos of you," which tells Google+ to try to find photos in which you've already been *tagged* (page 113)—an unlikely occurrence at this early stage—and "From your phone," which leads you through installing Google+ on your smartphone. That's quite a lot of work at this stage, though, and since you can change this photo at any time, just pick something fairly decent and upload it.

> **TIP** If you have a camera built into your computer and use Firefox, Chrome, or Safari as your web browser, you might see a "Web camera" option on the left of the picture-choosing box. If you like, go ahead and try taking a headshot using your webcam, but it can be tough to get a decently lit shot that shows your best side.

Once you choose a photo, Google+ displays controls that let you crop and rotate the image right in your web browser. Drag the four little white boxes to select the part of the image you want to use as your profile photo. You generally want to choose just your face, or perhaps your head and shoulders, so that your friends and acquaintances will be able to pick you out even if they're looking at a tiny version of your profile photo. Far-off shots of your handstands at the beach won't quite do (man, you really had a time in St. Lucia, didn't you?). If you need to rotate the photo, click the icons to the right of the image to spin it left or right.

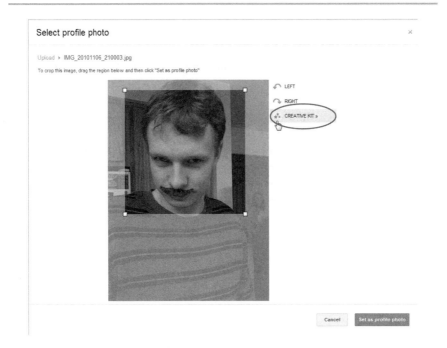

Need to do some serious tweaking to your photo? Click Creative Kit to edit it with a slightly customized version of Picnik, an image-editing program from Google that runs in your browser. When you do, the dialog box changes to include tools that let you adjust your photo in all kinds of ways. The four tabs at the top left let you choose from Basic Edits (like adjusting exposure and sharpening your image), Effects (such as adding filters or shapes), Vandalize (drawing, moustaches, and other goofy stuff) and Text (which, not surprisingly, lets you add text). You may see other options, too, depending on the season—like Halloween right around October 31. Click the icon that looks like a little gear if you want to work on your image in full-screen mode or access Picnik's Help files.

> **TIP** You're not restricted to using Picnik just on your profile photo. You can access its powers anytime to improve any photo, without even signing up for an account, at *www.picnik.com*.

When your profile image looks good, click the "Set as profile photo" button, and you'll land back on the profile-setup page. Now's a good time to take note of two notices on this page.

One is a checkbox that's automatically turned on. If you leave it on, you're agreeing to let Google use information from your Google+ account to "personalize content and ads on non-Google websites." That sounds like a pretty big thing to just casually allow the world's most powerful online-advertising firm to have access to, right?

You can click the ? icon after this disclaimer for more info. In short, what Google wants to do is allow websites that aren't part of the Google universe to install Google+ buttons, toolbars, and the like, and make them work with your Google+ profile. For example, when you read an article online or view a friends' photo on a photo-sharing site, you may see a little Google-styled +1 button (you learn more about how the +1 tool works starting on page 60). If you click that button, other Google+ members you're connected to will see that you like the article or photo. In addition, you might see online ads for stuff related to what you've given a +1. For instance, if you give a +1 to an article about a kitten getting rescued from a tree, you might start seeing ads for kitten chow, scratching posts, and the like on sites that use Google's ad-display services. If the thought of personalized advertising creeps you out, then turn off this checkbox—and don't click any +1 buttons you find around the Web.

The other caveat informs you that Google+ is in beta. That just means that you're a guinea pig and that some Google+ features may not work properly. The paragraph also makes it clear that you, not Google, are responsible if any data you didn't want to share somehow leaks out. So use common sense and don't put anything on Google+ that you wouldn't be comfortable sharing with your mom or your boss. (You can read the full Google+ privacy policy at *www. google.com/intl/en/+/policy*.)

With all that understood, you're ready to click the Join button and get going for real. Once you do that, Google+ displays a page that asks you to find people you know on Google+ through your Hotmail or Yahoo Mail accounts. If you use either of those web-based email services, you can click the "Find people" button next to its name, enter your email password, and then add people to your list of Google+ contacts right away. But, as explained on page 24, you can look people up this way at any time, so for now, go ahead and click Skip.

NOTE After you click Join, you may also see a message box offering to link Google+ with your Picasa Web Albums (this box only appears if you've already posted some photos on Picasa). Google is warning you that it's going to make it possible for you to share photos you stored in Picasa Web Albums through Google+ (though it won't share them until you say so), and start putting photos you upload to Google+ into your Picasa stash. However, albums you set up with strict privacy settings remain private. And, as a nice bonus, you get quite a bit more space on Picasa, because Google will stop counting photos under a certain resolution (2048 x 2048, to be exact) and videos under 15 minutes toward your total allotment of Google storage. For most amateur photographers, that means an unlimited amount of space. You can check your storage usage, by the way, by visiting *www.google. com/accounts/ManageStorage*. You *have* to click the "Link Google+ with Picasa Web" to continue into Google+, as clicking Cancel sends you back to the previous screen.

Next you'll see a page that lists some "interesting and famous" people whose posts you might like to read. These folks are shown in a grid on the left side of the page, and you can switch to a different category of people by clicking the topics on the right—entertainment, news, music, and so on. If you don't want to add anyone, just click Continue at the bottom of the page. If you happen to see someone you're interested in, mouse over the "Add to circles" button next to their name, pick Following from the list that appears under your cursor, and then click the Continue button at the bottom of the page. (You'll learn all about circles—including what the Following circle is and what public posts are—in Chapter 2.)

> **NOTE** If you decide not to connect with people in your email address book or with famous types, Google+ may display a pop-out warning that "You might be lonely." Just click "Continue anyway," and forget about Google's concerns. You can easily add people to your Google+ network from lots of places, as you'll soon see.

Fleshing Out Your Profile

YOU CAN JOIN GOOGLE+ by providing nothing more than your first name, last name, gender, and (maybe) birthdate, but it's better to give your friends and the folks who run across your profile more to go on. So the second page you see after officially joining Google+ is one where you can add details to your profile.

Add additional profile information to your public profile.
Adding more information will help your friends, family, and others find and connect with you.

School	Rock n' Roll High School	1999
Where you work	Bluth Company	Manager, Banana Stand
Where you live	The OC|	

Upload a photo from your computer or take a picture with your webcam.

Change profile photo

The fields on this page aren't mandatory, but they are pretty standard for most social-networking sites (and even most job applications): the school you graduated from, the place you work, and where you live. Why would you want to fill in these fields if they're not required? The box on page 11 gives you the lowdown.

After clicking "Continue" on the "Add additional profile information..." page, you'll arrive at the main Google+ screen, which shows—well, not a whole lot. That's because you haven't connected with anybody on Google+ yet, and with just a small portion of your profile filled out, folks might not instantly find you. Not to worry—that'll change soon. Head to your profile page by clicking the Profile button in the gray row of buttons near the top of this screen—it has a small head silhouette in a circle on it.

When you arrive at your profile, Google+ displays a white box that includes a few fields you can fill in to include a tagline and more details about yourself, like your employment and education history. Take note of the gray boxes under each of the profile pieces, including your photo. Click one of them, and you'll see a bunch of visibility options:

- **Anyone on the web** means just what it sounds like—anyone who searches for your name, stumbles across your profile page, or receives the web address for your profile can see those elements of your profile with this setting. This is the option Google+ chooses automatically unless you change it.

- **Extended circles** and **Your circles** are things you'll learn about in the next chapter. (Circles are the way you organize your Google+ contacts.) For now, consider these settings to mean "People I've specifically allowed to see this and/or friends of those people."

- **Only you** is just you, baby, and it's the safest option if you're not sure whether to share something. Google+ is, however, a *social* network, and so keeping stuff to yourself doesn't make it worth much.

- **Custom** lets you share info with particular people and circles. You'll learn how on page 55.

You'll have a better understanding of circles and Google+ sharing very soon, but for now, decide what you're comfortable leaving public, and set the other bits as "Only you" or "Your circles" (which, at this point, contain only you).

What a Google Profile Does for You

Why should I incude anything beyond the required basics in my Google+ profile? What's the point of letting strangers know where I've lived or sharing "bragging rights" with people I already know?

The answer, in part, is that the whole point of social networking sites—like Google+ and Facebook—is defining who you are, what you're into, and how you're doing to people you know and people you're just meeting. But another big reason is because the profile you're filling out in Google+ is the same one people may find when they search you out on the Web. It's just a fact

of modern life that people are likely searching for your name on the Web (probably via Google. com).

In the past, the answer to the question "How can I control what people see when they Google my name?" was "You can't," or perhaps "It requires a lot of work and/or a lot of money." Your Google+ profile (which is the same thing as your Google profile) gives you a kind of official response when someone Googles your name—a specially marked link to your profile. For example, someone searching out Devon Kurdy might see mentions of him in blog posts, his Facebook

–continued–

profile, and perhaps an unfortunate reference to him in a police report from his confused punk-rock period in the late '90s. But they'd also see a somewhat differently marked link to Devon's official Google profile, as shown here, so they can at least see what he has to say about where he's at these days before they read about his part in that 1998 Dead Kennedys after-party.

Your Google profile may not always be the first search result when someone Googles your name, especially if your name is very common, but it usually shows up on the first page of results.

Google

devon kurdy

Advanced search

Search

About 12,500 results (0.26 seconds)

Everything

Images

Maps

Videos

News

Shopping

More

▸ **Devon Kurdy** - Google+
https://plus.google.com/115084836407878595153 +1
Devon Kurdy - I tap and click things to describe how others should tap and click.

Picasa Web Albums - **Devon Kurdy**
https://picasaweb.google.com/115084836407878595153 +1
Devon Kurdy's Gallery · Profile Photos. Album for profile photos. Aug 2 ...

Profile Photos - **Devon Kurdy** - Picasa Web Albums
https://picasaweb.google.com/.../ProfilePhotos#5636291079685066... +1
Aug 2, 2011 – Photos by **Devon Kurdy**, Aug 2, 2011 - Album for profile photos.

Once you've entered what you want on your profile screen (it's all optional), click "Continue to my profile." If you've already clicked somewhere else, you can quickly jump to your profile from any page in Google+ by clicking the aptly named Profile button shown on page 10. It's one of the buttons at the top of every page, to the left of the search bar.

Your Profile page includes your name, your tagline (if you entered one), and your profile photo. Below your name and tagline are five tabs you can check out: Posts, About, Photos, Videos, and +1's.

Editing Your Profile

The section you care about right now is About, which is the first page people will see when they find you on Google+. If the word "About" below your name isn't in red text, click "About" to select it and see the information you've already provided. Then, click the blue Edit Profile button in the page's upper right to get cracking.

Change photo

Posts   About   Photos   Videos   +1's

Introduction

B *I* <u>U</u> Link

Just a dude with a Word template and a pair of sunglasses that reveals the secret alien conspiracy to get us all to consume and obey.

In Devon's circles (25)

View all »

Have Devon in circles (45)

Your circles ▾

Save   Cancel

Other profiles
What pages are about you?

Contributor to
What pages feature your work?

Recommended links
What pages interest you?

A red bar appears near the top of the page to indicate that you're editing, and when you move your cursor around the screen, whatever you're pointing at gets highlighted in light blue. When you click, a box pops up so you can edit that particular bit of info. Exactly how you edit each of these sections differs slightly, but there are a couple of aspects they all have in common: A text box (which is usually filled with some italicized placeholder text to provide inspiration) where you enter your info, and a gray box with the visibility options described back on page 10 where you decide who can see each bit of your profile.

With these tools, you can create different versions of your profile for different contexts. For example, you might fill out just a few boxes of very basic information—current employer, a generic tagline—and make those visible to "Anyone on the web." You can then add other, more personal bits—like "Bragging rights," places you've lived, and your relationship status—and make them visible only to "Your circles" or "Extended circles," which you can think of as "friends" and "friends of friends," respectively. Because you can control who sees which portion of your profile, you don't need to fill in generic, "safe" information that's boring and unhelpful to people who might be interested; just restrict the juicy bits to the people you trust. But you might want to hold off on entering things like your home and work contact information until you have a few contacts and circles in place (see Chapter 2); then, you can use the "Custom" visibility option to choose exactly who can see this sensitive info.

Change who is visible here

Some sections of your profile aren't just text, however. Below your profile picture, you may see small images of people you've added to circles, and people who have added you—but it's likely sparse, because you likely haven't added anybody yet if you're just getting started. Like everything else on your profile page, if you've clicked Edit Profile, this space includes a small globe icon you can click to change who can see your Google+ connections.

(Starting to see a trend? One of the major selling points of Google+, especially compared to other social-networking sites like Facebook, is the fine-grained control it gives you over who can see what, under what circumstances. Facebook has some settings to control stuff like this, but Google+ makes it clear what you're letting friends, acquaintances, and complete strangers see.)

Most of the other fields on your profile are fairly self-explanatory, but here are a few that aren't quite as obvious:

- **Send an email.** Clicking this setting displays an "Allow people to email you from a link on your profile" checkbox. Turning on this box lets people who view your profile click the "Send an email" button and send a message to the address you used to sign up for Google+—but people who click this button never see your actual email address.

- **Add some photos here.** Click this field, which appears below your name and tagline if you haven't added any photos yet (and you probably haven't), and you can upload photos from your computer (or, if available, photos from your Picasa Web Albums—see page 111) to give viewers a look at who you are and what kinds of pants you own. The process is the same as the one you used to select your profile photo (page 5); click the Add Photo square to get started.

- **Links.** On the right side of your profile, three different sections let you show folks your work and interests, and give you a chance to link up other accounts:

○ **"Other profiles" and connected accounts.** When you click the "Other profiles" link, a box pops up that includes two options: "Add custom link" and "Manage connected accounts." The first is a simple way to add a link to other sites where you maintain an account and post things regularly—like your blog or a forum you comment on frequently, for example. But if you regularly use Facebook, LinkedIn, or another online service, click "Manage connected accounts" to display a page that lets you connect your Google+ account to your other online accounts. You'll learn more about importing contacts from other networks into Google+ in the next chapter, but for now, feel free to add links to your Facebook profile, LinkedIn resume, or other types of accounts listed here (click the "Connect an account" button to see more options). Doing so makes info in those other accounts show up in your Google web searches, and to make it easier to identify and add people you know on other sites to your Google+ circles.

○ **"Contributor to" and "Recommended links":** Click either of these links if you want to add links to your favorite websites to your profile. You'll see two text boxes: Label and URL. Type a description of the site or its name in the Label field (*FC Buffalo Soccer*, for example) and the web address in the URL field (*www.fcbuffalo.org*).

• **Other names.** You'll find this item near the bottom of your profile page. If people know you by a name other than the one you signed up for Google+ with—professionally, before marriage, or for any old reason—entering it here makes it easier for friends to find you, and gives your profile more context when people are searching you out.

• **Profile discovery.** This important setting is at the very bottom of your profile—click it to see the "Help others discover my profile in search results" checkbox. Leave this setting turned on if you want your profile to be part of the results people see when they search for your name using Google and other search engines. Turn it off if you'd rather this profile not be visible to people searching you out on Google.com or other search engines.

TIP You can also decide which tabs you want to include in the gray bar that lists Posts, About, and so on. The first two tabs—Posts and About—are always visible; you can't turn them off. But if you click the Photos, Videos, or +1's tab while editing your profile, you'll see a "Show this tab on your profile" checkbox; turn it off to hide that particular tab from everyone, or turn it on to display the tab. (Alas, you can't set custom visibility options for these tabs like you can with other sections of your profile—it's all or nothing.)

All done editing? Mouse up to the red bar at the top of your profile and click "Done editing."

If all the buttons on Google+ were as clearly labeled as the "Done editing" button, this book could be mighty short. Luckily for your humble author, the "View profile as" box in the upper right of your profile provides just the kind of mystery this book can solve.

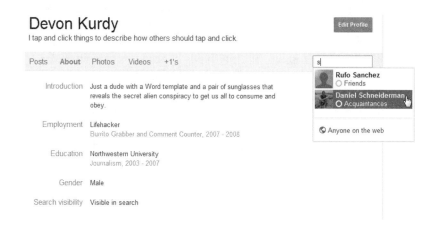

This box lets you test out all the visibility options you set up for your profile page. Click it, and then click the "Anyone on the web" option that appears in the drop-down menu. Your profile page will re-load to show what people without any special connection to you can see. (The one exception is the red "Viewing profile as" bar that appears at the top of your profile, which no one besides you can see.)

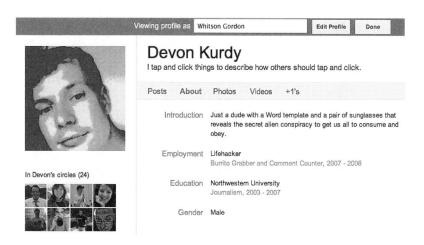

If you already have a few people in your circles, you can start typing someone's name in the "Viewing profile as" box on the red bar, and then select their name when it appears in the drop-down list to preview what that person can see. It almost goes without saying what a good idea it is to use this feature to preview what bosses, editors, overbearing friends, and all those other question marks in your social networks can see.

If you're comfortable with what appears in the preview, click the Done button. Otherwise, click Edit Profile to take another crack at tweaking your visibility settings. Then preview how your profile looks to various people until you're comfortable with who can see what.

Congratulations—you're officially on Google+! You'll definitely want to come back and edit your profile again as you add people to your circles, start using Google+ a bit more publicly, and learn more about how the site works. For now, though, you've got a profile that lets your friends find you, gives strangers just enough information, and keeps your misguided attempt at *Lost* fan fiction from dominating the Google search results for your name.

> **NOTE** If you own or manage a business, brand, or organization that wants to have a presence on Google+, you can do that as long as you've already set up a regular Google+ account. For the lowdown on setting up Pages—a new feature that lets companies and other groups connect to people on Google+—head to this book's Missing CD page at *www.missingmanuals.com/cds*.

Now that you're up and running with a Google+ account and a profile, you've likely got a few questions about what circles are and how they work. Luckily, circles are the subject of the next chapter.

CHAPTER 2

Managing Contacts with Circles

NOW THAT YOU'VE GOT YOUR PROFILE SET UP, you're ready to explore *circles*, the heart of Google+. Circles are groups of contacts that you organize however you like. You can give your circles whatever names make sense to you, since the people in them can't see these names. You probably already make circles in your head whenever you're looking to make plans: the friends with young kids who probably aren't free, the friends who don't get along with each other, the friends who live in another city, the relatives who are loving and dear but almost certainly won't fit in with your friends who obsess over *True Blood*.

> **NOTE** Other people can't see who you put in which of your circles (unless you intentionally share a circle, as explained on page 35), but they *can* see the people you're connected with on Google+—unless you hide this info. Page 14 explains how.

Circles let you easily share info with folks who actually care about it, and let you restrict sensitive tidbits to just a trusted few. For example, when you're dying to tell the world about the amazing new coffee blend you discovered at your local roaster, you can write a post about it and then share that post only with your Foodies and Friends circles, knowing that coworkers in the Better Future Corp. circle look down on such frivolity. Likewise, you can be sure when you're looking through posts by people in your Friends circle that you won't see any research summaries on cybernetic limb enhancement, and that many a cute nephew pic awaits you in your Family circle. You can let your Best Friends circle see all the photos from your Silly Pantsapalooza '11 weekend, while giving your Book Club circle a peek at just one (notably cropped) shot of you sitting by the campfire.

You don't *have* to create circles to use Google+. You could post updates and photos using the Public setting (explained on page 55), making them visible to anyone who's added you to their own Google+ circles *and* anyone on the Web who has sought you out. Or you could selectively share certain things with certain people, typing out their names and cherry-picking them for each update (page 57 explains how to do this). But circles help make sense of who can see your profile, posts, and photos. In effect, circles create multiple versions of your Google+ account—the Friends version, the Grandchildren version, the Design School version, and so on—that you customize for each group with your custom-grouped circles And maybe the best part of circles is that nobody sees them except you—so feel free to create a Never Really Liked circle for folks you only grudgingly interact with. This chapter explains everything you need to know about creating and managing circles.

How Circles Work

WHEN YOU FIRST JOIN Google+, the site provides you with four circles that you can use if you want. (If you don't like Google+'s circle suggestions, you can ignore, delete, or rename them.) To see these suggestions, head to your Circles page by clicking the Circles icon at the top of any Google+ page.

Google's suggested circles give you an idea of how you might organize the people you're connecting to on Google+. You can point to each circle to see a description of it. Here's how you might want to use each one:

- **Friends.** This circle is a good start, but you'll likely want to create separate circles for close friends who know all your deep dark secrets and for friends you know from very specific contexts.

- **Family.** Again, this circle may be a bit too all-encompassing, since not all family members fit into one big container, let alone at one Thanksgiving table. For example, you may want separate circles for your siblings and for your in-laws.

- **Acquaintances.** You may not find this circle very useful. Why? Because, acquaintances aren't as close as friends, so if you post something that you want to share with everyone, you may as well just make it visible to every-one on the Web.

- **Following.** Google+ suggests using this circle in a way similar to the Follow feature on Twitter. You can add people to this circle so you can see their posts, even if you've never met those folks personally. (Think celebrities and politicians.) But in contrast to Twitter, where you can see every tweet posted by the people you're following, on Google+ you only see these people's *public* posts (unless they've added you to one of their circles and are sharing with that circle).

NOTE   There is a way for people in your Following circle to see what you post (page 59 has the details). But it's unlikely that popular figures you add to this circle will see your posts, or even that you've added them to a circle, so it's pretty safe to assume that this circle is a one-way street: You can see public posts by people in this circle, but they likely won't ever read stuff written by little ol' you.

Why not just put a few relatives in the Family circle, dump everybody else into Friends, and move on? You could do that, but you'd miss out on the advantages of sorting folks into circles. The following section explains more about how cir-cles work; after reading it, you'll likely understand the allure of circles.

Deciding Who to Share With

You have multiple interests, certain views that don't conform to what people might expect, and people you know through particular interests or activities. Similarly, you're probably not interested in *everything* your friends are interested in. For example, you and your buddy from the softball team might have remarkably compatible views on 80's synth-pop and the best sushi in Brooklyn, but your politics might not align in the slightest. This doesn't come up in face-to-face meetings, because you've both learned each other's boundaries. But if you started a newsletter or blog that you filled with all your current political opinions and sent it out to friends like this, it would probably put an uncomfortable chill on your relationships.

This gets at the heart of what circles are meant to do. When you want to share something—a photo, a link to a web page, a "check-in" showing where you are, or just a quick note—circles make it easy to share it with exactly the right people. For example, you could upload photo 3,437 of your newborn and share it with your Family circle, the Friends With Kids circle you created to solicit parenting advice, and maybe even your Sorority Sisters circle for some bragging rights. The people in those circles will see your bundle of joy—but the folks in your Coworkers, Indianapolis, and Neighbors circles won't.

When you view your Google+ Home page (click the Google+ logo at the top of the screen to hop there), you get the other side of the coin: You see posts written by the people in your circles that they've shared either publicly or with a circle *they* put you in. So what do you do with that one friend who's kinda funny but who constantly complains about "tragedies" like high-end fashion boutiques not having the exact handbag she's looking for? You have two options: You can view only posts from circles you've created for more curated posts and less conspicuous consumption, or you can add her to a circle named something like Blabbers, and then only visit that circle when you feel like expanding your angst horizons. (Chapter 3 explains how to view posts from specific circles.)

Circles also let you have focused conversations with a select group of people. Creating a circle like "Race for the Cure Marketing Team," makes it easy to send links, updates, and photos to your team, and even have group text-messaging or video-chat sessions with them, without letting anybody in on the conversation who doesn't need to be there.

Perhaps the most important thing to know about circles is that you can assign people to *multiple* circles. For example, you could add your buddy Steve to your Los Angeles, Church, and Coffee Snobs circles. That way, if you post something about the City of Angels, an announcement for members of your congregation, *or* a link to a site that sells the single-source, shade-grown Arabica you're loving, Steve will be sure to see it.

Adding People to Circles

NOW THAT YOU KNOW how circles work, you're probably itching to start organizing the people you know into circles. The best way to get started is to click the Circles button (pictured back on page 20) at the top of whatever Google+ screen you're on.

If you're truly new to the Google universe (you don't use Gmail, for example) and just created your Google account as explained in Chapter 1, your Circles page will look like the one here. (You can practically hear the crickets.) But if you use Yahoo's email service, Hotmail, or a desktop email program and have a sizable contact list built up, you can import those contacts into Google+ and see if anyone you know is already on the site (the box on the next page explains how). Even if they're not, you can still share posts and photos with them by having Google+ send them emails; page 57 explains how.

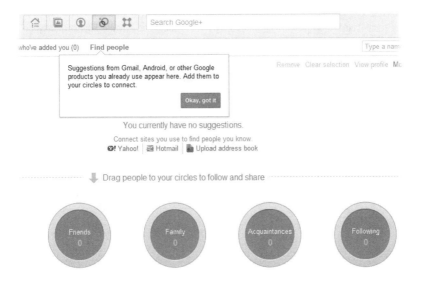

Importing Contacts

Google+ makes it easy to import lists of folks you already correspond with so you can add them to circles. To get started, head to the Circles page and click the "Find people" heading. When you do, the screen changes to display three icons labeled Yahoo, Hotmail, and "Upload address book." If you use Yahoo or Hotmail, click the appropriate icon to bring up a new browser window where you can type in your username and password for that service. You then need to confirm that you want to give Google access to your Yahoo or Hotmail address book. Once you give your permission, if any of the contacts in that account are signed up for Google+ or simply have a Google account, you'll see them in the "Find people" section of the Circles page.

Another option is to upload an address book from Outlook, Apple Mail, or some other desktop or web-based email program. Nearly every email program can export contacts as either a comma-separated values (.csv) file or a vCard (.vcf) file, and Google+ can understand both formats. Exactly how you export an address book depends on your email program, but it's usually pretty simple. In most versions of Outlook, for example, you'll find an Export option somewhere on the File menu. If you use Mail on a Mac, launch Address Book, select all your contacts, and then drag them onto your desktop to create a vCard file containing all their details. With your exported contact file handy, head to Google+'s Circles page and click the "Upload address book" icon. In the dialog box that appears, find the .csv or .vcf file you created and double-click it. Any of your contacts who are on Google+ will appear on the Circles page.

If you have some contacts built up in your Google account because you've been using Gmail, Google Chat, or some other Google service, you might see a few familiar faces on the Circles page. (If you don't see anyone, click "Find people" near the top of the page.) These are folks who you've either previously contacted, or people Google *thinks* you might be connected to because you have a number of contacts in common.

TIP   You can whittle down the list of people in the middle of the Circles screen by clicking "People in your circles" or "People who've added you" in the screen's upper left. You probably won't see anyone if you click "People in your circles" since you're just getting started, but you might see a few if you click "People who've added you," especially if a friend invited you to join Google+. Yup, strange as it may seem, people can actually add you to their circles before you join the site.

Don't see any names at all, or don't see the people you want to add? No problem. In the upper right of the Circles page, click the "Type a name" box, and then start entering the name of someone you know. As you type, Google+ displays potential matches, automatically updating its suggestions with every letter you type. The most relevant names should appear near the top—people who know one of your existing contacts (if you have any), people who live near you, people who've worked at the same companies as you, and so on.

If you see the person you're looking for, double-click her name to jump to her profile page just to make extra sure you've found the right person. (Nothing's more embarrassing than adding someone to one of your circles and then having that person contact you to ask, "Who the heck are you?") The information you see in the profile is limited to things that she's set as visible to "Anyone on the web" (just as you can set the visibility of items in your own profile; see page 10). If the profile belongs to someone you know, go ahead and click the "Add to circles" button in the upper right of her profile, and then flip to page 27 for details about how to select the circle(s) you want to put her in.

NOTE On Gina's profile, and on the profiles of other folks of note, the gray checkmark next to her name (circled here) means that Google "verified" her name, giving you and others a thumbs-up that this person is, in fact, using her real name and is the person most people know by that name. (If you hover your cursor over the checkmark, it expands to read "verified name.") Who gets a verification badge from Google? Celebrities, public figures, and people added to an especially large number of circles. So keep an eye out for these checkmarks when you're looking for a profile that belongs to your favorite actor, musician, or other notable person.

How does Google verify that the Dolly Parton on Google+ is really the country music legend? They're not telling. Gina Trapani notes that Google didn't email, call, or contact her to verify her account, so the process remains a mystery. But unless you become a celebrity, you probably won't get verified by Google+.

If you don't see the person you're looking for, don't give up just yet. In the Search Google+ box that's at the top of every Google+ screen, type the person's name. A drop-down list appears with "Search Google+ for X" as the first option, followed by the same profile pictures and names that showed up when you used the "Type a name" box. Below that is a section titled "Searches" that contains some suggestions of search terms that might help you find the person you're after.

Clicking one of these phrases or the "Search Google+ for X" option makes Google+ search its *entire* network, not just its database of names. So if someone mentioned the person you're looking for in a post, or they were cited in a photo, or they show up anywhere else, you might see them in these search results. If the results include the person you're looking for, you can click her name or photo to view her profile.

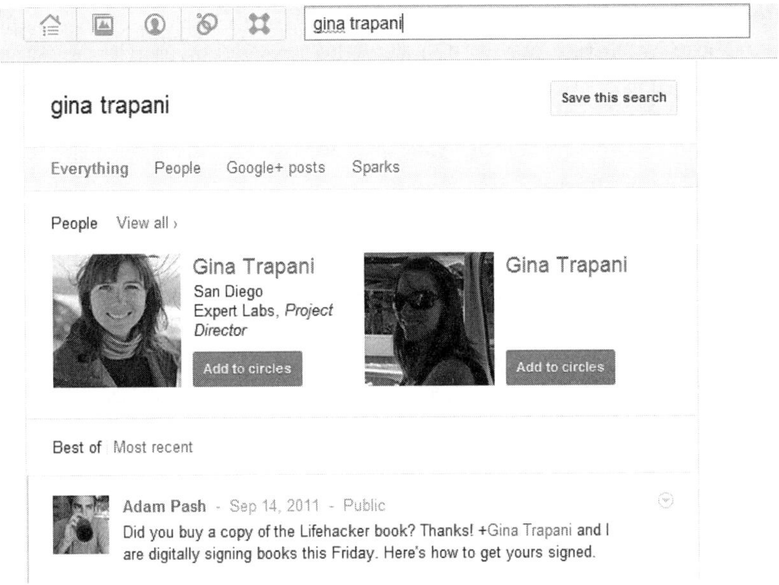

gina trapani   Save this search

Everything   People   Google+ posts   Sparks

People   View all ›

Gina Trapani
San Diego
Expert Labs, *Project Director*
Add to circles

Gina Trapani
Add to circles

Best of   Most recent

Adam Pash - Sep 14, 2011 - Public
Did you buy a copy of the Lifehacker book? Thanks! +Gina Trapani and I
are digitally signing books this Friday. Here's how to get yours signed.

Putting People in Circles

Now that you've found someone you want to put in one (or more) of your circles,
adding that person to a circle is easy. Google+ gives you a few ways to do this,
as the following sections explain.

From a profile page

If someone's not in one of your circles yet, at the top right of his profile page
you'll see a big red "Add to circles" button, as shown here. When you point to it
with your cursor, Google+ displays a list of
your existing circles. (This list probably only
includes the four pre-fab ones you read
about on page 21, but you'll learn how to
create your own on page 30.) To add someone to one of these circles, just click the
name of the one you want to add him to.
Simple, huh?

☐ Friends	0
☐ Family	0
☐ Acquaintances	0
☐ Following	0
Create new circle	

From the Circles page

You can also add people to circles by heading to the Circles page shown on page 23; click the Circles button at the top of any Google+ page to get there. If there are a bunch of boxes in the middle of the screen with people's names (and maybe photos) on them, you can add one of those people to an existing circle simply by dragging his box onto one of the blue circles at the bottom of the page. (The circle expands so you can tell that it's selected and, if there are any people already in it, you see their profile pictures around the edge.) Let go of your mouse button to add him to that circle.

Drag people

Drop here to create a new circle

Rufo Sanchez

Friends

8

See a bunch of people you want to add to the same circle? Click one person's name box, and then simply click another, and another, and so on. Each box you click turns blue to indicate that it's selected.

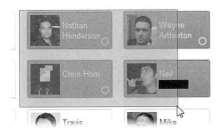

Another way to select multiple people is to click somewhere between the boxes in the middle of the Circles page and then drag to create a selection box, as shown to the left of this sentence. Keep holding your mouse button until the box contains everyone you want to add to a circle. When you let go, Google+ selects all the people within the selection box. (Chances are that a few people you don't want to include will get caught up in the selection box. No problem: Just click the boxes of anyone you don't want to add to the circle to deselect those people.)

TIP   To double-check who's included in the currently selected batch of people, click the Selected header near the top of the Circles page. It's smart to do this just to make extra sure you haven't accidentally included Grandma in the group of people you plan to add to your Scandanavian Death Metal Fans circle. If someone you don't want is part of the selected group, simply click her name box to exclude her.

Once you've got several people selected, click one of the blue, selected boxes and drag it toward a circle. That box and all the other selected ones will collapse into a cute little paper-clipped pile of people, with the total number shown on a folder-style label. (Wouldn't it be easy to plan movie night if people really lined up like this?) When you let go of your mouse, Google+ adds all those folks to the circle you selected.

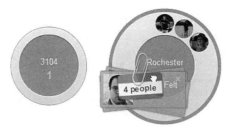

If you don't see anyone listed on the Circles page, type a name into the Search Google+ box at the top of the page. If the person you're looking for appears in the drop-down list, simply drag her name from that list onto the appropriate circle at the bottom of the page.

TIP The Search Google+ box is also handy for sorting through your contacts if you have a ton of 'em. So rather than scrolling up and down on the Circles page to find someone in the list of people boxes, just type his name in the box and, when he appears in the drop-down list below the box, drag him into a circle.

Creating Circles

IF THE FRIENDS, FAMILY, Acquaintances, and Following circles that come with Google+ don't match the way you'd like to organize the people you know, no problem. You can create your own circles using any of these methods:

- **On someone's profile page,** put your cursor over the red "Add to circles" button and then click the "Create new circle" link that appears. Google+ displays a text box so you can name your new circle. Type a name and then click Create to add that person to that circle.

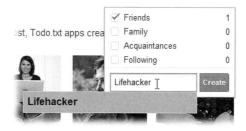

NOTE If person whose profile page you're viewing is already in one of your circles, you won't see the "Add to circles" button. In its place, you'll see a green button labeled with the name of the circle you put her in or, if she's in more than one of your circles, the green button will say "2 circles" (or "3 circles," or whatever). No matter what the button looks like, pointing your cursor at it will display the list shown in the previous illustration, with checkmarks next to the circles she's in.

- **On the Circles page,** you have two ways to create a new circle:

  - Drag a person's name box onto the circle that's labeled "Drop contacts here to create a new circle" (you can also select several name boxes and drag one of them onto the "Drop contacts here" circle to add them all in one fell swoop). That person (or those people) will orbit inside the in-progress circle until you click the "Create circle" link inside it. (If you change your mind and decide not to create the circle, or start over, click the Clear link instead.) When you click "Create circle," you'll see a new window pop out, where you can name the circle, give it a description (mostly so you can remember the reason for its existence), and add many more people quickly by searching them out.

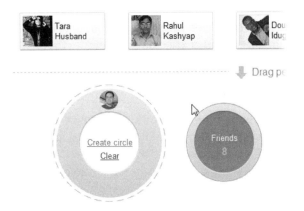

  - Click the circle labeled "Drop contacts here to create a new circle" (it changes to display a "Create circle" link). Google+ displays a dialog box where you can type a name for the circle and a description, and add people. To add someone, click the "Add a new person" box and then start typing a name; when the person you want appears in the list of suggestions, click her name to put her in this circle. Once you've added everyone you want in this circle, click the "Create circle with" button, which lists the number of people you've added. (If you'd rather add people to this circle by dragging their boxes on the Circles page, click the "Create empty circle" button instead.)

How-To Geek

Nerds I know that write for the obsessive how-to site (a.k.a. "Ask These People for Windows Advice") Edit description

People to add   Search in this circle 🔍

Sort by: Relevance ▾   Remove Clear selection

➕ Add a new person   Lowell Heddings

Jason Fitzpatrick

Jason Fitzpatrick

Jason Fitzpatrick
Four Leaf Films LLC

Cancel   Create circle with 1 person

Types of Circles to Consider

You should create whatever circles work for you. The way you use Google+ may be different from everyone else, and you may end up setting everything you post as visible to all your circles or everyone on the Web. But if you want more fine-grained control of who you share with, here are a few types of circles you could set up:

- **Location-based.** Sometimes you really *do* want to tell everybody you know how great the weather is in your neck of the woods. But your friends in Baltimore probably don't care about the awesome cupcake shop you just found in Portland, Maine. So it might make sense to create separate Baltimore and Portland circles.

- **Work groups, volunteer groups, and so on.** If you work with people on projects, Google+ is a great way to share resources and comments—and even communicate in real time. Add the people you work with on various projects to project-specific circles to start the conversation.

- **Casual groups.** Maybe you meet up with a small crew every day, week, or month to have coffee, try a new restaurant, or take in a movie. Wouldn't it be nice to relive jokes, expand on ideas, or just trade gossip between sessions? Create a circle for each group to do just that.

- **Sensitive and tricky types.** Some people just can't resist the temptation to comment on, question, or raise a ruckus over every little thing. You don't *have* to create circles like Powder Kegs, Gossips, Irritable Conservatives, or Sensitive Liberals, but if you do, the people you add to them would never know and you might save yourself some headaches. Having circles like these will prevent you from simply posting everything to all your circles, but it's worth that inconvenience to avoid having those people post head-shaking comments.

- **More-specific Following circles.** Rather than just adding everyone you're interested in hearing from to the generic Following circle (page 21), consider creating separate circles for your specific interests: Cooking, News, Technology, Music, and so on.

You may not need all this differentiation in your Google+ account, but circles are free and you can create as many as you want, and having a lot of them isn't usually a bother, so you may want to try adding a few to see whether they work for you. You can always delete the ones you don't end up using.

Editing and Organizing Circles

THE CIRCLES PAGE MAKES it easy to organize your social contacts. To get started putting everything in its place, put your cursor over a circle at the bottom of the page. When you do, the circle expands and, in the gray ring around the outside, you see the headshots of up to a dozen of the people in that circle. Next to the circle, a message box appears that lists the total number of members in that circle.

TIP To delete someone from a circle that you're pointing to on the Circles page, simply click the person's headshot in the gray ring and drag their picture off the circle.

For the four circles Google provides (Friends, Family, Acquaintances, and Following), the message box also includes a description, but you don't have to stick with it. To edit that description or do more in-depth circle editing, click anywhere in the blue center of the circle. When you do, the circle flies up to the top half of the Circles page, where you'll see boxes for each of the people in that circle. (You can tell which circle's members are displayed because Google+ puts the name of the circle above the boxes.)

The circle you clicked turns gray, and Edit, Delete, and Share links appear in it. Clicking Edit displays a small box, where you can change the circle's name and description. The Delete link does just what you'd expect—deletes that circle. But deleting a circle only deletes the circle itself. You can always find the people in it again (page 24), and those people won't be removed from any other circles you put them in.

Near the top left of the Circles page, above all the people boxes, is a "Sort by" drop-down menu that lets you change the order in which Google+ sorts the people in this circle. Click this menu and you can choose to sort folks by first name, last name, relevance (explained in the following Note), or the order in which you added them. To find more people to add to this circle, you can use the "Type a name" box just above these contacts on the right, which instantly shows other people you might want to add to this circle below the list of folks already there, as quickly as you can type. Simply drag those name boxes that appear onto the appropriate circle, as explained on page 28.

NOTE How does Google+ sort your contacts by "relevance," exactly? The folks at Google aren't telling, but it seems to be based on whether you've had other interactions with those people via other Google services (you've traded messages in Gmail, for example, shared photos through Picasa Web Albums, or what have you). This sorting option doesn't necessarily work too well for everyone, so try other options to sort through people and find new circle additions.

Just as on the main Circles page, you can double-click a person's name box to see her profile, and select multiple people by clicking them in succession or drawing a box around them. Your changes are saved automatically as you move people around.

That's how you manage the name, description, and roster of a circle, but how do you organize your circles themselves? Say you want to give a few circles priority placement when they show up in various Google+ lists and on the Circles page? You do that the same way you organize people on Google+: by dragging them around.

At the bottom of the Circles page, drag any circle in your collection to reposition it so that it's in a higher position and easier to access when it's time to add people or choose a group to check on. As shown here a faint gray line indicates where the circle will end up when you release your mouse.

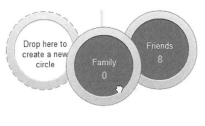

TIP Need some more space to figure how to arrange your circles? Put your cursor over the dotted gray line between your contacts and circles, and the cursor turns into two arrows with one or two horizontal lines between them. When you see that cursor, drag to move the divider between your contacts and your circles to provide more room for either section.

Sharing Circles

YOU'VE LEARNED ALL ABOUT creating, naming, and organizing circles, and you might never want to let people see some of your circles (like Sexist Salespeople, for instance). But maybe you've created a great "Chefs on Google+" circle and want to share it with all your fellow foodies. You can do that pretty easily.

At the bottom of the Circles page, click the circle you want to share so that its members are shown in boxes near the top of the page. On the right side of the page, you'll see links for removing people, viewing profiles—and a "Share this circle" link.

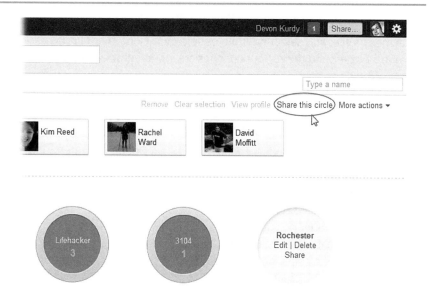

When you click this link, you'll see a box asking which of your circles you want to share this circle with (sounds like a recipe for motion sickness). You can also add a comment, which you should definitely provide so that the people you're sharing with know why you think they should add a whole group of people they probably don't know to a new circle.

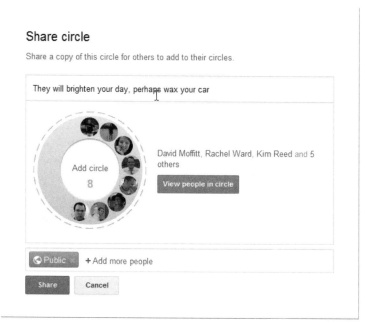

When you click Share, you'll be prompted to choose which other circles or people you want to share your circle members with. Note that it's just the members of the circle you're sharing, in a bundle—your name for the circle isn't revealed. The people you shared the circle with will see it in their streams You'll learn more about what people see when you share things with your circles in the next chapter.

CHAPTER 3

Streams, Sharing, and Privacy

THE *STREAM* IS THE HEART OF GOOGLE+: It's where you go to check out the stuff that connects you to the people you know. It's where your friends, family, acquaintances, and all the other people you added to circles share their thoughts and lives—and you do, too. Photos, links to websites, funny one-liners, longer pieces of writing—they all go into the stream. But you control where your posts go: who can see them, and even who those people can share your items with. And you get to choose what items you see from which circles of friends.

This chapter explains how to navigate and enjoy your stream: viewing what other people are up to and interested in; writing about your own experiences; and responding to the posts of friends, acquaintances, and complete strangers, even if only to give them a quick "+1" high-five. Once you know how it works, you'll find that it's quite easy to learn a lot about people in Google+.

Viewing Your Stream

GETTING TO YOUR MAIN stream is easy—it's where you land whenever you log into Google+. Simply head to *www.plus.google.com*. If you're already logged into your Google account, you'll see your main stream immediately. If not, click the red Sign In button, enter your email address and password, and then click "Sign in"—voilà, your main stream!

TIP If you're using another Google service like Gmail or Google Docs, you can jump to your main stream by clicking the "+[your first name]" link on the left side of the black bar at the top of any Google page.

If you're already in Google+, click the Google+ logo or Home button near the top of any page to see your main stream, which includes posts from all the people in all your circles.

Your stream is the busiest part of Google+. Think of it like a lobby in a college dorm with a big bulletin board where people have posted all kinds of messages, pictures, and notes about what they're doing, where they've been, and so on. Viewing the stream for just a particular circle (which you'll learn how to do in a sec) is akin to moving from the lobby of the dorm into a hallway, where you'll (likely) to run into only the people who live there—in other words, the people in that circle. Unlike in college, though, you have a lot of control over who has access to each hallway, and you have the power to mute or boot bad or boring stuff.

The Anatomy of a Stream

WHETHER YOU'RE LOOKING AT your main stream or the stream for a particular circle, the Stream page includes the same basic features.

On the left is your profile image and first name (click either one to bring up your profile page.) Below that is a list that indicates what stream you're looking at. This list includes all your circles, plus a couple of other items you'll learn about momentarily: Incoming and Notifications. You can read about the Incoming stream in the box on page 59, and Chapter 4 covers notifications. (If you have a lot of circles, you'll also see a More link in this list, which you can click to view all your circles; when you do, the link changes to a Less link that you can click to collapse the list again.) If you're looking at your main stream, the word "Stream" at the top of this list is in bold, red text. If you want to view a sub-stream that includes only posts by people in a specific circle, click that circle's name in this list.

The center of the Stream page is where all the action happens. At the very top is a title that indicates which stream you're looking at: It says "Stream" if you're looking at your main stream, "Friends" if you're looking at your Friends stream, and so on (this title is the same as the item selected in the list on the left side of the page). Just below that is a box prompting you to "Share what's new." You'll learn all about this box starting on page 46.

> **NOTE** If your circles aren't very full or if your contacts aren't all that active on Google+, you might see a "Not enough posts in your stream?" link section below the Share box. Ignore it if you're just trying things out. Clicking the red "Find people" button takes you to the same page where you search out contacts and invite them to join Google+ (shown on page 4).

Below the Share box is the top-most post in this stream. The items in the stream *aren't* simply in chronological order (though newer posts are generally near the top of the list). Nope, Google+ deems some posts more important than others and bumps them up in the stream. Which ones? Google hasn't given away the exact formula it uses, but posts that have a lot of *comments* (page 62), have received quite a few *+1* votes (page 60), and have been *shared* for greater exposure (page 64) tend to move up the list. And any post that specifically mentions you jumps up to a high spot in your stream. But even posts that pick up continual clicks and attention slide down the stream after a while. Page 62 explains posts in more detail.

TIP   You can scroll through the posts in a stream in several ways: by using your mouse to drag your browser's scrollbar, pressing your keyboard's up and down arrow keys or Page Up and Page Down keys, or even by hitting the J and K keys (see page 78 for more keyboard shortcuts).

Main Stream vs. Circle Streams

The *main stream* is the one you see immediately after you log into Google+, or when you click the Home button (page 40). In the center are posts from *everybody* in all your circles. You can tell you're looking at your main stream because the word "Stream" appears in red on the left of the page, and in black at the top of the page (circled on page 41).

The big difference between your main stream and the streams for your various circles is which posts you see: Your main stream includes posts by all the people in your circles, while the stream for a specific circle only includes posts by the people in that circle. Another difference is what appears on the right side of the page. When viewing your main stream, here's what appears in the right-hand column:

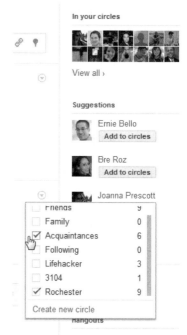

- An **In your circles** section that includes thumbnails of your friends' profile photos, with a "View all" link beneath them. Clicking a person's image takes you to their profile, while clicking the "View all" link zips you to the Circles page (page 20).

- A **Suggestions** section that includes thumbnails of people Google+ thinks you might want to add to your circles. These folks can appear for a few different reasons: You've contacted them via Gmail, friends in your circles have added them to their own circles, or they live in the same area or have worked for the same company as you, for example. (They're the same suggestions you see in the "Find people" section of the Circle page.) If you see someone you know and want to quickly add them, simply mouse over the "Add to circles" box under their name, and a small box listing all your circles appears. Scroll through and turn on the checkboxes for the circle(s) you want to add her to (or click Create new circle), and then simply mouse away when you're done.

- The **Send invitations** section includes a button for sending invitations to friends who aren't on Google+ yet. The box on page 4 has the details.

- The **Hangouts** section is related to, well, *hangouts*, which you'll learn about in Chapter 6.

- The **Games** section (which may or may not show up) shows you several of the games that you can play on Google+. Chapter 9 has the skinny on Google+ games.

- The **Google+ Pages** section links to a spot where you can create a Page for a business, brand, organization, or another public entity. You can find more info about Pages on this book's Missing CD page at *www.missingmanuals. com/cds*.

NOTE Google+ is constantly changing. This chapter describes how the streams pages looked while this book was being written, but it's possible you'll see different things on the right side of your stream pages.

Click the name of a circle on the left side of the Stream page, and the page will change in a few major ways. Most importantly, the center column now shows only posts by people in that circle.

Friends (9)

Your real friends, the ones you feel comfortable sharing private details with.

+ Add to Friends

View all

Circle sharing

Recommend the people in this circle to others.

Share this circle

On the right side of the stream page, a few other things have changed, too. The top item is now specific to the circle you selected: It includes the name of the circle, how many people are in it, the circle's description, and thumbnails of some of the people in it. Beneath the thumbnails is an "Add to [circle name]" box. Click this box and start typing a name, and matching Google+ members (and contacts from your Google account, if applicable) appear in a drop-down list. Click a name to add that person to the circle whose stream you're viewing.

Below that you may see the same Suggestions section described previously. There's also a "Circle sharing" section that includes a tempting green button. Clicking it lets you show the people in any of your circles to the people in any other circle, all your circles, or the public. (Circle sharing is covered in detail on page 35.) Below that is the Hangouts section described above, and in the bottom right of your screen is the "Send feedback" button described next.

The Feedback Button

As of this writing, Google+ is still pretty new and technically in *beta* (available for people to use, but with no promises about everything working properly). In order to help improve the site, Google makes it easy for you to weigh in with suggestions, complaints, and other kinds of observations by including a gray "Send feedback" button in the bottom-right corner of every Google+ screen. Click it, and you'll get a pretty cool tool for telling Google when something goes wrong on the site, or if there's something that you just don't like about Google+. A box pops up that includes two buttons: Highlight and "Black out."

The Highlight button is automatically selected. With this button turned on, you can move your cursor over a section of your screen to point it out to Google (you can highlight several different parts of the screen if you want). If your screen includes something you don't want the people at Google to see like a friend's phone number, click the "Black out" button and then click the thing you want to hide.

In the "Describe the problem" box, explain the bug you've discovered as specifically as you can. When you're done, click the Preview button to see the information that will be sent to Google. If you want to make changes, click Cancel to get back to your original screen and start again. If everything looks okay, click "Send feedback to Google."

Go ahead and use this handy feedback tool whenever you feel irked or like something must be broken. The folks who created Google+ will honestly appreciate it.

What's In a Post

Every post includes the same basic features:

- **The poster's profile photo and name.** Click either one to hop to that person's profile page.

- **The time and date the post was published.** (If the post was created today, you see only the time.) Click this timestamp to see the post on a separate page.

NOTE You may see the term "(edited)" after a post's timestamp, which means that the person who wrote the post made changes to it after she originally posted it. Page 66 explains how to edit your own posts.

- **The word "Public" or "Limited."** This indicates whether this post is available for the whole world to see or restricted to just a worthy few. To see exactly who a limited post was shared with, click the word "Limited" to display a pop-out box with thumbnails of up to 22 of the other people who can see it.

- **A faint gray arrow inside a circle.** Click this icon to see a menu that lets you link to the post (page 69), report abusive content in the post to Google, "mute" the post, or block the person who posted it, so you won't see any further posts from him (all covered on page 70).

 Adam Pash - Aug 24, 2011 - Public

Simple tricks-of-the-trade stuff is always among my favorite @lifehacker posts—like this one http://goo.gl/gkkto

Knot Your Power Cords Like a Carpenter to Avoid Unwanted Unplugging

 If you've ever used an extension cord, you've no doubt experienced the heartache (yes, heartache!) of pulling a few inches too far and disconnecting from the cord.

NOTE You may see another item after a post's timestamp: the word "Mobile," or maybe "+1'd on [something.com]." This lets you know that the post was written by someone using Google+ on their cellphone or mobile device, or was typed by someone who clicked a +1 button on a website other than Google+. In either case, it's just to let you know that the post was probably typed quickly or on a small screen so you'll be more understanding of brevity and typos.

Below all that is the meat of the post: whatever the person typed when he created the post. If he included a link to something (like the knot-tying article mentioned in the post shown on page 45), a preview of the web page he linked to appears below what he wrote: a sample photo from his latest photo album, a still from the YouTube video he pointed to, or a small slice of a map showing where he "checked in," for example. You'll get a better sense of what to look for in a post when you write one of your own.

Now you know how to view different streams and decipher posts, and you're probably eager to do something besides just *look* at stuff. You'll learn how to interact with other people's posts later in this chapter (page 60). For now, it's time to learn how to write your inaugural post.

Writing a Google+ Post

ONCE YOU'VE WRITTEN A POST, shared it, and seen how it shows up in a stream, you'll have a better sense of how the whole stream thing works. Plus, writing a post is a great way to announce yourself to the Google+ universe, and then you can watch the comments and approving +1s (page 60) roll in.

To get started, head to your main stream page (if you're not already there) by clicking the Google+ logo or the Home button near the top of the screen, and then click the "Share what's new" box. The box expands to give you plenty of room to type. Decide what you want to tell everybody, and then type it in ("Hello world!" is always a good start). You may automatically see a blue rectangle labeled "Your circles" appear below where you're typing; if not, click the "Add people or circles to share with" box and select "Your circles." When you're done, click the Share button. Congratulations—you've just written your first post and shared it with everyone in your Google+ circles!

Adding Photos, Videos, Links, and Locations

The icons in the lower-right of the "Share what's new" box let you add extras to a post: a photo (or photos), a video, a web link, and your location. However, you can add only one of these extra elements to each post—a set of photos, a video, *or* a link. The one exception to this rule is that you can add a location to any post.

These extras can be a subtle footnote to the text you write in the "Share what's new" box, or the text can serve as a caption for—or description of—the extra. For example, you could write a long post that thanks everybody for coming out to your fundraising event, and then attach a crowd shot to demonstrate the success; or you could write a short note about the event, and then attach a series of photos showing highlights of the night. Most links needs *some* kind of explanation—at least a blurb about why you find a site interesting or relevant—but most videos don't need lots of text, as they usually speak for themselves.

Here's how to add each kind of goodie:

- **Photos.** Click the camera icon and a menu with three options appears. Click "Add photos" to browse your computer and select the photo(s) you want to upload; click "Create an album" to upload photos in a more organized fashion by dragging and dropping the files into the order you want; or click "From your phone" to post images from your smartphone (you need the Google+ app to do this; see page 107 for details). Photos need to be in JPG, PNG, or GIF format, and no larger than 2048 pixels on their longest side (about 2 MB). You'll learn more about sharing photos in Chapter 5.

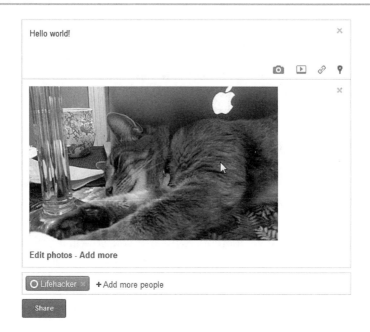

Hello world!

Edit photos · Add more

Lifehacker + Add more people

Share

- **Video.** Click this icon, which looks sort of like a play button, to display a menu of three options. Choosing "Upload video" lets you do just that—upload a clip directly from your computer. You can upload videos in nearly any format (though you'll get the best results with MPEG-2, MPEG-4, and H.264 files), but they need to be smaller than 1 GB and less than 10 minutes long. Click the YouTube option to bring up the "Choose a YouTube video" dialog box, where you can type in a search term or the name of the video you're looking for (type *keyboard cat*, for example, to add that catchy gem to your post). The third option is "From your phone," which, as with photos, you need the Google+ app to use.

- **Link.** This icon is supposed to resemble a couple links of chain (get it?). When you click it, a text box appears so you can type out or paste in a link to a website. You don't have to type *http://www* at the beginning—*oreilly.com* or *npr.org* works just fine. Once you hit Enter or click "Add," your link shows up at the bottom of your post, with the title of the web page, a short description of it (pulled from the text of the page), and a thumbnail image. You can click the arrows at the top of the thumbnail to choose from other images on the page you linked, or click the X to not include an image. Similarly, you can click "Remove description" to axe the text under the link; it's good to provide some context for the page, but not if it's gobbledygook.

Stream

Nothing about this fishbowl isn't amazing   ✕

                                                    📷 ▶️ 🔗 📍

◉ FISHSCAPE FISHBOWL ($100-200)   ✕

◀ ▶ ✕   FISHSCAPE FISHBOWL, $100-200, available at
               blessthisstuff.com
                                          ⬚

Remove description

🌐 Public ✕   + Add more people   ▾

- **Location.** You don't have to type, paste, or select anything to add this
  extra—simply click the red icon that looks like the place markers used in
  Google Maps, and Google+ determines your current location automatically. The location may be very specific, with GPS-like coordinates, or more
  general, like "Omaha, NE."

  "Wait," you might be asking, "my web browser knows where I am?" Yes,
  but not unless you give your browser, and whatever site is asking, permission to estimate your location, and not in any particularly scary way. Most
  modern web browsers—Chrome, Firefox, Safari, and newer versions of
  Internet Explorer—let websites politely ask for your location. So when you
  click the Location icon, you may see a message from your web browser
  asking if it's okay for Google+ to figure out your whereabouts. If you agree,
  the site pulls in information about your *IP address* (the unique string of
  numbers assigned to your computer by your Internet service provider) and
  (if you're using a wireless connection) the details of your WiFi router. With
  these numbers, Google+ can usually figure out what neighborhood you're
  in. (If you're using a mobile device that connects to cellular towers and has
  a GPS chip, the location is much more specific; Chapter 8 has more info.)

  As noted above, you can add a location to a post even if you've already
  added photos, a video, or a link.

TIP If you get partway through a post and then decide you don't want to include that photo, video,
or link anymore, click the X button in the upper-right corner of the extra's box to wipe the slate clean
and remove the extra you attached. To remove your location, click the X on the right side of the thin
location box.

Posting on Google+, or any social networking site, is a good way to learn how to best convey your sentiments. As you experiment, you'll learn what gets a reaction (positive or negative) from your friends and contacts. If you want to get a discussion going, for example, pose a semi-open question: "What do you listen to when you've got a whole lot of household chores to crank through?" That works a lot better usually than just posting "Ugh, chores!" The same goes for photos, videos, and links—the more informative and interesting they are, the more likely you'll get responses and have your posts shared more widely (page 64).

NOTE You can also post to Google+ from a text message sent to a special number. See Chapter 8 (page 188) for details on writing posts via text message.

Mentioning People in Posts

You can casually mention people in your posts as much as you like: "Mom just made the best peach pie!" or "Just got back from hanging out with my buddy Jim—good times!" But, confusingly, Google+ uses the term *mention* to mean something really specific: directly addressing another Google+ member, or even a friend who hasn't joined the site yet, by including her name in a post with a + character before it. This comes in handy when you want to bring someone's attention to a post, and perhaps give other people reading your post a link to the tagged person's Google+ profile. You can do that by mentioning the person in context ("*+Adam Pash* and I are huge fans of AeroPress coffee," for example), or by tossing someone's name in at the end ("AeroPress coffee is always amazing! *+Adam Pash*").

When you mention someone in a post, in addition to seeing your post in her stream, the person you mentioned also gets notified about the post (exactly what form the notification takes depends on her settings; see Chapter 4 for details). (If she's *not* signed up for Google+, Google+ sends her an email notification.) Also, her Google+ name (which links to her Google+ profile) is visible—and clickable—to whomever else you share the post with, unless she's blocked them (the next section covers sharing options in detail; page 69 explains blocking). So, your friend who likes to keep a low profile online might not appreciate you mentioning her in your posts.

To tag someone in a post, type either @ or +, and then start typing the person's name. In the list of suggestions that appears, click her name or, if the right name is highlighted in the list, just hit the space bar or Enter key (Return on a Mac).

Stream

TIP If you aren't trying to mention someone, but instead just want to type a term that includes the @ or + symbol, when the list of suggested names appears, press the Esc key or click somewhere besides the list to make the list disappear.

You can mention people who aren't in your circles, and even people who haven't added you to their own circles, and they'll see the post in their main stream. Do that too often or in an invasive kind of way, however, and the person you mentioned might block you (page 69). Also note that, when you mention somebody in a post, Google+ adds their name to the list of people and circles the post is shared with, and that you *can't* remove her. (Probably Google+'s way of making sure you don't say mean things about people.)

If you want to get really advanced, you can include *hashtags* in your posts, just like on Twitter. To learn about hashtags and how to add them to your posts, flip to page 164.

NOTE As of this writing, Google+ is working with other companies on tools that will let you write posts and manage various aspects of Google+ without having to go to the Google+ website or install the Google+ mobile app (see Chapter 8). Some of these tools will make it easier to post things to Google+, Facebook, Twitter, and other services simultaneously. For more information about the status of these tools, head to this book's Missing CD page at *www.missingmanuals.com/cds*.

Choosing Who Sees Your Posts

AFTER YOU'VE WRITTEN THE text of your post and added any extras you want to include, it's time to decide exactly who you want to share it with. The box above the Share button (the one with the placeholder text that begins with "+Add") is where you determine who's lucky enough to have access to your brilliant witticism, piece of news, or whatever you're sharing. Before you learn exactly how to use this box to control the visibility of your posts, it's helpful to get an overview of what it means to share with different circles and groups of people.

You may have used other social networking sites to share things with friends (on Facebook) or followers (on Twitter). Google+ is different from those kinds of sites because of the sharing and privacy controls it gives you. On Facebook and Twitter, everything you share is visible to everyone you're connected to on the site and/or everyone on the entire Internet. In Google+, on the other hand, you create circles, your friends and contacts create circles, and the things you see in your streams represent where those circles overlap. You can share with just a few people or with everyone online, but the circles and streams are where all the interesting ideas, links, photos, and sharing happens. The idea of restricting your posts to certain people or circles may sound confusing, but it's the kind of thing you do every day in emails, in huddled conversations, and in addressing particular groups. Here's a concrete example:

You, Bob, and Rachel are all Google+ members. You and your friend Bob share a love of restaurants and fancy food pictures. Rachel is a work acquaintance you don't know quite as well, but you know she loves books about management, leadership, and motivation, with titles like "Getting There Innoventually."

You add Bob to your Foodies circle, since you two share that interest. You add Rachel to your Forced Acquaintance circle (remember, no one but you sees the names you give to your circles).

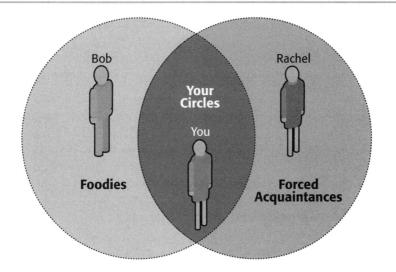

After organizing your circles, you decide to post a cute picture of your cat, Butterscotch, curled up next to some liquor that's still sitting out from last night's little gathering. Now you have to choose who to share it with. You know it's not a good idea to share photos that include booze with all your circles (since your parents might see it) or everyone on the Internet (since your boss might see it), so you want to choose a specific subset of your Google+ friends. Bob was at the shindig and will probably like the picture, but Rachel tends to spend her evenings crunching at the gym, cleaning out her work inbox, and planning her action items for the next day, so she probably won't be amused by Butterscotch's antics. So you share the photo with your Foodies circle.

Does Bob see it? Yes—*if* he's added you to one of his circles and he looks at his main stream, since that stream includes all the posts from everyone in all of his circles. However, if Bob has created a circle that you're not in called Feline-Free Friends, when he browses through that circle's stream (which he does by clicking Feline-Free Friends on the left side of his Stream page), he won't see Butterscotch there. But if he looks at the stream for the Gourmands circle he added you to, then he'll see the snapshot. (This is a good example of how you can use your various streams to filter whose posts you see.)

TIP So, what if you add Bob to a circle, but he hasn't added you to any of his? Then Bob won't see most of your posts. The only cases where he will see them are if a mutual friend of yours and Bob's shares your post (page 64), if you mention Bob in the post (page 50), or you specifically add him to the list of people and circles you're sharing the post with. But otherwise, Bob's streams will be mostly free of your posts, though he'll continue to show up in your streams.

Rachel, on the other hand, doesn't see the picture of Butterscotch and the bottle of crème de cacao because you intentionally didn't send it her way. She won't see your adorable orange furball *even* if she's added you her "Professional Contacts to Synergize and Conquer" circle or she goes out of her way to click your profile to see what you've posted recently.

So remember, there are two sides to the whole circles thing: the circles *you* arrange your friends into, and the circles *your friends* create and put you in. You control your own circles, but there's no way of knowing what kinds of circles other people have put you into. So all you need to worry about is deciding which circle(s) to share with, as explained in the next section.

Post Visibility Options

Now that you have a general overview of the ways you can share with certain groups of people, it's time to learn how to actually pick those groups in Google+. These visibility options let you share items with only the people who will truly appreciate them.

As the following sections explain, Google+ tries to be smart by automatically choosing a group to share your post with based on which stream you're viewing while you write it, but you can always choose a different group if you want.

Writing a post while viewing your main stream

On your main stream page, below the text of your post and any extras you added, is a box that reads "+Add circles or people to share with." If you shared your last post with "Your circles," Google+ automatically puts "Your circles" in this box again. If you shared your last post with some other group of folks or you don't want to share this post with everyone in all your circles, you have to select the people and circles you want to share with.

Edit photos - Add more

+Add circles or people to share with...

Share

To be more selective about who you share with, click the "+Add circles or people to share with" box. A menu appears that includes several options. The text at the top of the menu explains that you can type a person's name or email address to share just with that person, or type the name of the circle you want to share with. Here's what the other options are for:

Type or select a circle or person. Or
just enter an email address.

Friends (4)

Family (3)

Acquaintances (1)

Following (0)

Your circles

Extended circles

Public

- **Specific circles.** At the top of the menu are the names of your circles. If
  you have more than three or four circles, you'll also see a "# more" link that
  indicate how many other circles you have that aren't shown in the list; click
  this link to see the names of *all* your circles. To select the circle you want to
  share with, click its name in this list or type its name in the +Add box.

TIP   The first three circles you see listed in this menu are the ones in the upper left of the circles
section of your Circles page (covered in Chapter 2). Changing the order they appear in this list is a
simple matter of heading to your Circles page and then dragging your most important circles to the
first three slots.

- **Your circles.** This means that your post will be shared with everyone in
  all your circles. If you share that picture of Butterscotch with this group,
  both Bob and Rachel will likely see it in their main Google+ streams,
  which include everything posted by everybody in their circles. In addition, Bob will see it in his Gourmands stream, and Rachel will see it in her
  "Professional Contacts to Synergize and Conquer" stream.

- **Extended circles.** This option is something of an odd duck. It includes
  all the people in all your circles *and* all the people in *their* circles. It's the
  Google+ equivalent of "friends of friends," except that your posts appear
  in the Incoming streams of the people in your friends' circles. (The box on
  page 59 has more about this stream.)

- **Public.** If you cropped that photo of Butterscotch so that it showed nothing
  but your fuzzy feline, then you'd have no reason not to post it for the whole
  world to see. In that case, you could post it using the Public setting. Doing
  that sends the post to all your Google+ contacts *and* makes it visible to
  everyone on Google+ *and* on the whole Internet. That means that a friend

of yours could copy and paste the timestamp from your post (see page 65 for details), send it out in an email, post it to their blog, or otherwise distribute it, and *anybody* could look at it.

Posting something publicly isn't as scary as it may sound. It's a great option for people working in the media, building their personal or small business brand, or trying to get attention for their chosen topics. Public sharing is what people do on Twitter, and it's increasingly how Facebook wants its users to share their posts and photos. In Google+, it just means that you're sharing to everyone in your circles and other people could potentially find it on the Web.

When you select an option in this list, a corresponding blue or green rectangle appears in the +Add box. For example, if you have a Lifehacker circle and select it in the list of visibility options, a blue rectangle labeled "Lifehacker" appears in the +Add box, as shown here.

Edit photos - Add more

Lifehacker ×   +Add more people

Share

Writing a post while viewing a circle's stream

If you write your post while viewing a specific circle's stream, Google+ automatically puts a blue rectangle representing that circle in the +Add box because it assumes you want to share the post with that circle. If that's true, then you can just leave the +Add box alone. But if you want to share with more people than just the ones in that circle, click "+Add more people" to do just that. You can also click the X that appears when you mouse over a circle or person's name to remove them from the sharing list.

Lifehacker (3) View all
Adam Pash, Gina Trapani,
Whitson Gordon
☐ Notify about this post

Lifehacker ×   +Add more people

Share

For a reminder of who's in that circle, point your cursor at the blue rectangle. If there are a bunch of people in that circle, you'll see the first few names, and you can see the rest by clicking the "View all" link at the top of the pop-up box. What about the "Notify about this post" checkbox? Normally, when you post to a specific circle, the people in that circle will see this post if they look at their main stream or the stream for whatever circle they put you in (like if Bob looks at the stream for his Gourmands circle, for example). If you turn on the "Notify about this post" checkbox, Google+ will *also* send the people you're sharing with a special alert about your post. Depending on their Google+ settings, that could mean they see a notification in their Google toolbars, receive an email, or hear a little bloop from their phone—something like, "Take note: Devon Kurdy wants you to see this post." (Chapter 4 has the details on notifications.)

NOTE
If you add someone who's not on Google+ to one of your circles, when you go to share a post with that circle, you'll see a checkbox next to the Share button labeled "Also email 1 person not yet using Google+." This checkbox is turned on automatically, and it's basically an attempt by Google+ to attract more users. Google is hoping that, when your friend gets an email letting him know about the post, he'll sign up for Google+ to see the brilliant insight you've written.

Other posting tips

Clicking the +Add box and selecting circles by clicking works okay if you've got less than, say, a dozen circles. But if you have more than that, the list becomes quite long and a bit cumbersome. Fortunately, there's an easier way to add circles: click the +Add box and then typing a few letters of the name of the circle you want. When the right one appears, hit Enter (Return on a Mac) or click its name in the list.

In addition to—or instead of—sharing with circles, you can share posts with individual people. For example, say you want to share news of your promotion with everyone in your Family circle and your buddy Bruce, or you just heard some gossip about your high school math teacher and want to share it with your three closest friends. To share with a specific person, click the +Add box and start typing her name, and Google+ will suggest matches.

The names of people who are already contacts of yours should appear at the top of the list, but what about the other folks listed? Those names are Google+'s guesses as to other Google+ members you might know. If a name looks familiar but you're not sure (or the name is something as common as John Smith), click the name to add that person. Then, click the person's name in the +Add box to see her profile.

TIP When you mention someone in a post, that person is automatically added to +Add box, and also, even if they're not? That's the point behind Google+ adding them automatically, right? You can't remove them, either. Google+ is old-fashioned that way—it won't let you go talking about somebody without their knowing it.

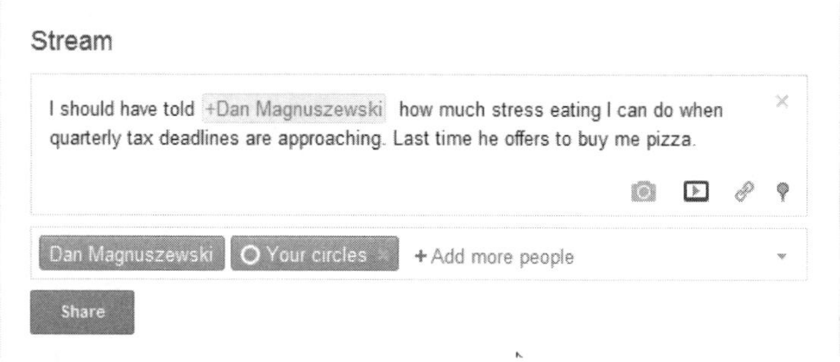

Stream

> I should have told +Dan Magnuszewski how much stress eating I can do when quarterly tax deadlines are approaching. Last time he offers to buy me pizza.
>
> 📷 ▶ 🔗 📍
>
> Dan Magnuszewski | O Your circles × | +Add more people ▾
>
> Share

If it turns out you don't know this particular John Smith, no problem. To delete a person or circle from the +Add box, click the X at the right end of the rectangle representing that person or circle.

When all the right people and circles are listed in the +Add box, click Share to send your post out to those people's streams.

The Incoming Stream

I don't see an Incoming circle on my Circles page, so what's the deal with the Incoming stream?

The Incoming stream is an anomaly in that it doesn't match up with a specific circle. (The other exceptions are your main stream—which shows posts from people in all your circles—and the Notifications stream, which only includes notifications [see Chapter 4].) Here are the kinds of posts that appear in your Incoming stream:

- **Posts by friends of friends.** As you learned on page 55, if someone who's connected to one of the people in your Google+ circles shares something and sets the visibility of that post to "Extended circles," it'll show up in this stream.

- **Posts specifically shared with you.** These are posts where people either selected your name in the +Add box or mentioned you

in the post (see page 50). You'll see these posts in your main stream, too.

- **One-sided posts.** As you've learned, the whole circles concept is a two-way street: You can add people to circles, and they can add you to circles. If you haven't added Bruce to any of your circles but he's put you in one of his, when he writes a post or *shares* someone else's post (see page 64), it'll show up in this stream.

Your Incoming stream will quickly get cluttered with posts by people you don't know, people who post too much stuff to too many people, and folks you haven't added to a circle. You might think that perusing this stream is a good way to find people and add them to your circles, but there's a specific section of the Circles page ("People who have added you") that serves this purpose far better; see page 23 for the details. So, overall, the Incoming stream isn't terribly useful for anything besides killing time.

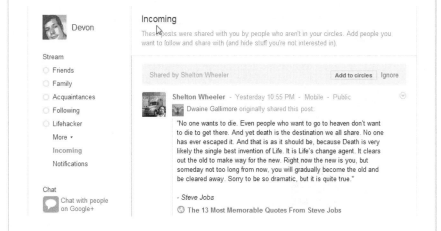

Interacting with Posts

NOW THAT YOU'VE SET up some circles and learned how to post to them, it's time to find out what you can do when you see stuff you like in your stream.

TIP If you see something you *don't* like in your stream, Google+ gives you a few different ways to respond. See page 69 for details.

Other people's posts are just like yours: they include some text, perhaps some mentions, and maybe an extra like a link, video, photo, or location. Hopefully you find some of them interesting—perhaps interesting enough to +1, comment on, or share that material with your own circles. The following sections explain each option.

The +1 Button

Giving someone's post a *+1* (pronounced "plus one", just like it looks) is the equivalent of a thumbs-up, a laugh with a smile, or a knowing nod—just a quick acknowledgement that you think the post is good, funny, poignant, worthwhile, or right up your alley. (The box on page 61 explains where the term "+1" came from.)

To give a post a +1, click the +1 button below the body of the post. When you do, you see a little animation that "rolls over" the total number of +1s that post has received, and the +1 button turns blue. If you're the first person to give the post a +1, the phrase "You +1'd this" appears below the +1 box. If others have already registered their +1 sentiments, you see a number below that box indicating the total number of +1s ("+24," for example).

Travis Hardiman - Jul 18, 2011 - Public
http://mrwhaite.tumblr.com/post/7649387534/neonpeewee

Mr Whaite, A neon poster for Pee-wee's Big Adventure....

A neon poster for Pee-wee's Big Adventure. Tequila!
http://youtu.be/BodXwAYeTfM

+1 - Comment - Share

+1

Other people who look at the post are able to see that you've given it a +1. To see who liked a post, click the blue +# link, and Google+ displays the little pop-up shown below.

Viewing other people's +1s

You might remember from the signup process that you could +1 items on pages outside Google+, and how that would lead to customized advertising (page 8). And, as you've just read, clicking +1 while on Google+ is a kind of stamp of approval. So where do all these +1 clicks end up? In a special section of your Profile page, and on everybody else's Profile pages, if they're made public.

If you want to show off your +1s, you have to edit your profile and make the +1 section of your profile visible: Head to your Profile page, click Edit Profile, click the +1's tab, and then turn on the "Show this tab on your profile" checkbox. Once that's done, folks who view your profile can view the things you've given a +1 to: web pages other than Google+ (by clicking a +1 button in a Google search result or on the page itself) and posts and photos on Google+.

FREQUENTLY ASKED QUESTION

The +1

Where did the term "+1" come from?

Google+ includes a +1 button for a few different reasons, all of them geeky.

In role-playing games, dating back to the pen-and-paper version of *Dungeons & Dragons*, a +1 indicated a rare, upgraded version of an item (like Broadsword +1, for example).

In computer programming, +1 is a common way of making a program run over and over again (such as, "If x does not equal 10, x=x+1 and run again until x=10").

And on web forums and in website comments, writing "+1" is the simple way of saying "Good show." So Google uses +1 for all those reasons—and the fact that Facebook had already laid claim to the Like button.

Bonus question and answer: Where does the + in Google+ come from? Google considers Google+ an "upgrade" of Google's other services, since it adds a social aspect to them.

Commenting

When you want to respond to a post with something more specific than a +1, click the Comment link next to the +1 button. (You can, of course, both comment on a post *and* give it a +1.) When you do, a text box appears so you can type your feedback.

You can do most of the same things in a comment that you can do in your own posts, like mention people or link to websites or videos—although you don't get the same icons or images as when you're writing your own post. You can't attach image or files from your computer to a comment, so if you want to write a really robust response to a post, your best bet is to start a brand-new post that includes a link to the original post (page 65 explains how), and then mentioning the original post's writer (page 50) in your post.

When you're ready to add your comment, click the "Post comment" button (hitting Enter (Return on a Mac) instead doesn't post your comment, it just adds a line break to what you've written).

TIP If you really want to keep your hands on the keyboard, you can hit the Tab key to select the "Post comment" button and *then* tap Enter (Return on a Mac) to add your comment.

If you post a comment and then decide that what you wrote wasn't quite right, click the Edit link below the comment. Doing so gives you full editing powers on your comment.

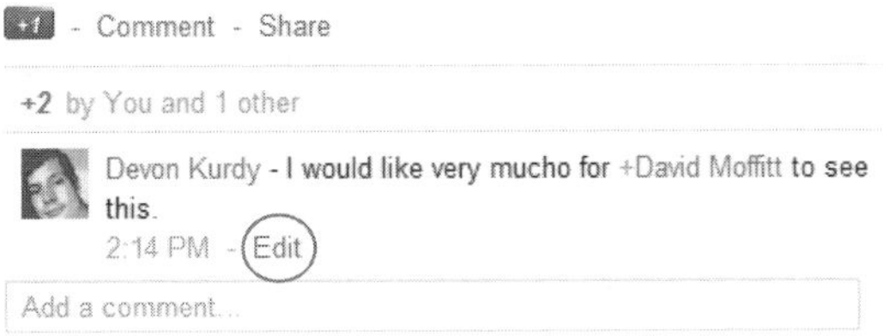

+1 - Comment - Share

+2 by You and 1 other

Devon Kurdy - I would like very mucho for +David Moffitt to see this.
2:14 PM - (Edit)

Add a comment...

If things went *really* wrong and you'd like to back out entirely, click "Delete comment." If you change your mind again and want to leave your comment as is, click Cancel. After you make changes and click "Save changes," Google+ updates your comment, changes the timestamp next to it to reflect when you made your changes, and adds "(edited)" next to the timestamp so folks know that you changed the wording.

+1 - Comment - Share

+2 by You and 1 other

I would like very mucho for +David Moffitt to see this.

| Save changes | Delete comment | Cancel |

Add a comment...

Posts aren't the only things you can give a +1 to. Sometimes the best thing about a post isn't the post itself, but another person's take on it. When you're looking at a post and point your cursor at a particular comment, you'll see a +1 button appear. To let everyone know how much you like that comment, click that button.

Rachel Ward - Aug 18, 2011 - Limited
WOAH. Straining Fage yogurt basically turns it into pudding.

+1 - Comment - Share

Jared Rutz - Greeks are strained enough already.
Aug 22, 2011 +1
Click to +1 this comment

Add a comment...

If a post has received several comments, you can see them all by clicking anywhere in the line that contains the double-arrow symbol, on the right side of the post's comments section (it looks like this » except it points down.)

Sharing Others' Posts

If someone writes a post that's good enough that you want to share with your friends, click the Share link below the post to send the text, link, or whatever else is in the post out to your circles. (Don't worry—the original author will get credit.) The pop-up that appears includes some of the same controls you see when you write a post from scratch, plus a text box at the top where you can type in an explanation of why you're re-posting this item.

NOTE   When you click the Share link, you may see a message box that says "This post was originally shared with a limited audience – remember to be thoughtful about who you share it with." See page 68 for details about this warning.

Share this post

Here's another first world problem: the typeface. So serif-y!   I

Whitson Gordon originally shared this post:

The first world problem to end all first world problems.

How to Plug In a USB Cable Correctly Every Time

Plug In USB   Doesn't fit, flip it.   Somehow, even if we think we know which direction that USB cable is supposed to plug in, you always second guess yourself when it doesn't go in the first time.

Doesn't fit, right again   Now it fits

Public   + Add more people

Share   Cancel

Unless it's entirely self-explanatory, it's a good idea to add a little note about why you're sharing a post. Without a note from you, people in your circles might be surprised to see a post from someone they don't know. It's kind of like bringing someone new to a gathering of friends—you should probably introduce him and explain how you know him.

Devon Kurdy · 1:02 PM · Limited
Here's another first world problem: the typeface. So serif-y!

Whitson Gordon originally shared this post:

The first world problem to end all first world problems.

How to Plug In a USB Cable Correctly Every Time

Somehow, even if we think we know which direction that USB cable is supposed to plug in, you always second guess yourself when it doesn't go in the first time.

+1 · Comment · Share

TIP   Clicking the Share link is the *official* means of sharing posts you like, but you can easily share a post via email, a blog post, or wherever. To do so, you need to copy the link from the post's timestamp. Right-click the time to the right of the poster's name (or, on a Mac, hold the ⌘ key and click), and choose "Copy link location," "Copy shortcut," or whatever similar option appears on the shortcut menu. You could also click the timestamp to bring the post up, by itself, in your browser, and then copy the link from your browser's address bar. Then you can paste that web address into any email, Facebook post, or wherever else you want by right-clicking and choosing Paste, or hitting Ctrl-V (⌘-V on a Mac). Take note, though, that the usual Google+ privacy policies apply: unless the person clicking the link is in the circle the post was originally shared with or the post is set to Public, he'll see a "Error: Page not found" message.

Editing, Deleting, and Controlling Your Posts

YOU MIGHT WONDER HOW valuable Google+'s circle, stream, and privacy controls are if the site lets anybody who can see your post share it with whoever they want. Well, you need not worry, as Google+ does place some restrictions on how far something can be shared.

If someone posts something with the Public visibility option, then you can share it with whoever you like. But it's a different story when someone attempts to share a post that you restricted to only a certain circle. Google+ gives you a few additional privacy controls that appear after you post something. To see them, click the gray arrow in a circle on the right side of your post. (If you don't see the post in your main stream, try clicking over to your Profile page, which includes a Posts section.) The drop-down menu that appears gives you some options for editing and restricting access to your post.

Devon Kurdy - 5:48 AM - Limited

My only regret is that I have but one hard
adorable cat pictures.

Or maybe more than one, depending on if

+1 - Comment - Share

Edit this post

Delete this post

Disable comments

Lock this post

Not every thought you type into Google+ is going to be gold. You might decide later on that you phrased something the wrong way, that you mentioned the wrong person, or that you don't want that post up at all. Or you might simply see a typo or bad link. Whatever the reason, select "Edit this post" in the drop-down menu to tweak the text of the post, or remove links, photos, or videos you included in it.

NOTE You can't *add* a location, video, or photo to a post when you're editing it—which can be somewhat aggravating. So if you want a post to declare your whereabouts or focus on a particular photo or video, you'll need to include those items from the get-go. You can, however, add links to a post you're editing.

Devon Kurdy - 5:49 AM (edited) - Limited

My only regret is that I have but one hard drive to give in service of adorable cat pictures.

Or maybe more than one, depending on if that SSD upgrade happens.

Save   Cancel

+1 - Comment - Share

Change whatever you want about the text or extras, and then click "Save." Just like when you edit comments you've written, your post will have a new time-stamp with "(edited)" appended to it. One thing you can't change when editing a post: the circles you initially shared it with. You can restrict how people in those circles are able to share your post (as explained in a moment), and share your post with *more* circles, but you can't un-share a post without deleting it entirely. On that note, "Delete this post" is the second option in the drop-down menu. When you delete a post, Google+ removes it from your stream and the streams of everyone you shared it with. But as you'll learn on page 68, deleting a post isn't the same as wiping the information it contained off the face of the earth. People may have spotted the post in their streams while it was up.

Controlling and Deleting Comments

The folks you share your posts with generally mean well. But sometimes their sense of humor and yours might not jibe. Or they may get into an argument in the comments of your post, or characterize aspects of what you posted in ways you don't appreciate. Fortunately, you have some control over what goes on in the comments of your posts. In the drop-down menu shown on page 68, choose Edit Post.

When you select this menu option, two icons appear at the right edge of each comment on your post when you mouse over them: an X and a flag. Click the X to remove the comment, or click the flag to remove the comment *and* report it to the Google+ team. You should only report a comment if you think it's spam (if it says "Low-cost electronics, iPads, Viagra!," for example) or an inappropriate or abusive remark that violates Google's terms of service (which basically state that you can't write anything hateful or obscene on the site). When you remove a comment, the person who wrote it receives a notification that you've done so. If you report a comment, the comment's author will hear from Google's community moderators, and, if the person gets reported a few times, likely get kicked off Google+ entirely.

> **TIP** If you want to head off bad comments at the pass, or prevent further clamor on a pointed post, you can choose "Disable comments" in the drop-down list instead. Doing so won't remove any of the comments that have *already* been written about a post—that you'll have to do manually as explained above—but it'll keep people from writing new ones. If you change your mind later, you can click the same arrow and choose "Enable comments."

Controlling Sharing

On page 64, you learned how to share a post written by a friend who's in one of your circles. When someone posts a link using the Public visibility setting (page 55), anyone can link to it and see it, so sharing is simple.

But when you're posting something to one of your hand-picked circles, you might not want to let those people share that post with the people in *their* circles. Just like with real-life storytelling and gossip-spreading, the results can sometimes turn an innocent quip or story into a great big drama. So Google+ includes two features that help keep sharing in check: a warning message and the ability to *lock* your posts.

When you post something to any group other than Public, if one of the people in your circles clicks that post's Share link, Google+ shows them a little reminder that you didn't share the post publicly, so you probably don't want it shared with the whole online world.

The message is basically there to remind folks to be considerate, and most people will. But you never know when somebody—perhaps that old coworker of yours who got fired over an email incident back at WidgeTech—is going to test the limits of social graces. Because Google+'s polite reminder may not dissuade everyone, if you post something of a sensitive nature, you can clamp down on casual sharing of it. To do so, click the little gray arrow in the upper-right corner of your post and choose "Lock this post." That way, your post won't include a Share link.

That means your friends can no longer share your post—at least not in the easy way they could before. But keep in mind that if you put something online, there's *always* a way for someone to share it in ways you don't want. Even if you disable sharing and comments and do your best to keep a post inside your selected circles, people can *still* share your stuff by:

- Copying the text of your post and then pasting it somewhere else in Google+, into an email, onto Facebook or Twitter, or wherever.

- Taking a screenshot of your post (by pressing PrtSc on a Windows computer or ⌘-Shift-3 on a Mac), cropping the image, then posting it somewhere.

- Telling other people about what you posted, whether on Google+, in person, or any other means.

So keep that in mind when you're thinking about posting something. And if you come across a locked post, the person who wrote it is very firmly asking that you don't share that joke, photo, or bit of humor with anyone else, even though you technically could.

Bottom line: If you *really* want to keep something private, don't post it on Google+ or anywhere else online.

Blocking, Muting, and Reporting Posts

Not every post in your stream will be a winner, and some you might get downright sick of because they keep jumping to the top of your stream as they collect comments and +1s. That's what that little arrow in the upper-right corner of each post is for—telling Google+ that a post is either too prominent or just plain bad, or that a person (probably someone who's not in your circles) is continually shoving posts into your stream and you'd like it to stop.

Whitson Gordon - Yesterday 7:50 PM - Public

An ode to LXDE/Lubuntu, my personal favo

Lubuntu Breathes New Life into You
Sacrificing the Flexibility of a Full-Fled

Netbooks aren't the
can be useful—as lo
want your netbook to
computer rather than a toy, I can't recommend
Lubuntu eno...

Link to this post

Report abuse

Mute this post

Block this person

Options menu

+1 - Comment - Share

+29
10 shares - Alwin Hawkins, Darren Moore, Garmon Estes, Harley Inb...

Click that arrow to display the Options menu, where you can choose from the following:

- **Link to this post.** If the post has been published as Public, when you select this option, Google+ opens a new tab in your browser (or a new window, depending on your browser settings) showing just this post. Then you can select the web address in your browser's address bar, copy it by pressing Ctrl+C (⌘-C on Mac), and then paste it wherever you'd like. It's much the same as copying the post's timestamp as explained in the Tip on page 65.

- **Report abuse.** If a post is obscene, abusive, intentionally aggravating, or just pure spam, click this option to display a "Report this post" box where you can detail what's wrong with the post.

Report this post

Thank you for helping Google by reporting content which may be in violation of our Community Standards.

Why are you reporting this post?

- ⦿ Spam
- ○ Nudity
- ○ Hate speech or violence
- ○ Child abuse
- ○ Copyright
- ○ Other

Cancel   Submit

- **Mute this post.** If a post keeps appearing at the top of your stream either because it's popular, it keeps getting updated, or it somehow triggers another of the signals Google+ uses to determine posts' relevance (page 41) and you're sick of seeing it, click this option. Doing so doesn't harm the reputation of the person who posted it nor does it delete the post itself, it simply removes the post from your stream. In its place, you'll see a thin bar noting that the post has been muted, with an "Undo mute" link you can click to bring it back.

- **Block this person.** This option is meant mainly for people who show up in your stream because they keep mentioning you (page 50), sharing specifically to you, or are somehow intruding on your Google+ experience. Blocking someone keeps you from seeing any more of their posts in your stream, no matter what they do to call your attention to them. They won't know that you've blocked them unless they do some serious investigating into why their shared posts and comments on your posts aren't showing up as they normally would.

  When you select this option, you see the box shown on page 71. It explains that blocking someone removes that person's ability to see and comment on things you post, you won't see the things you'd normally see from that person (like posts and comments), and she won't be in your circles anymore. When you post something as Public, she can still see that, but only if she happens across it somewhere outside her main Google+ stream. A new, red circle named Blocked will also appear on your Circles page; you can drag people into and out of it, just like regular circles.

What happens if you block Cassandra Rife

- You will no longer see this person's content in your stream.
- This person won't be able to comment on your content.
- This person will be removed from your circles.
- This person will still be able to see your public posts.

Cassandra Rife won't receive an email about these changes. You can always unblock this person later.

Cancel   Report and block this person   Block Cassandra Rife

Note there are two block buttons: "Report and block this person," and "Block Jane Doe." Click "Report and block" when that person has posted, commented, or otherwise behaved in a way you think is intentionally harmful, obnoxious, spam-like, or otherwise against the social norms, and you think they should be booted off the site for everyone's benefit. Click "Block Jane Doe" when you just don't want that person pestering you anymore.

CHAPTER 4

Notifications

LOTS OF STUFF CAN HAPPEN on Google+ when you're not looking. In between your visits to the site, people can +1 or comment on your posts and photos, or share them with their own circles. People you've never met can add you to their circles and folks you've added to your circles can add you back. And people can mention and tag you in posts and photos, send you messages, and so on. Google+ doesn't want you to miss any of this, so it uses *notifications* to let you know about these happenings even when you're not logged into the site.

When you first join Google+, you'll probably smile and get a little self-esteem boost every time you see a notification. But as your circles grow and your stream gets busier, you'll want to manage and scale back these notifications, or at least make them less intrusive. This chapter explains all the notifications you can get, where you can get them, and how to fine-tune them to hit the sweet spot of not missing anything important yet not feeling overwhelmed.

Where You Get Notifications

GOOGLE NOTIFICATIONS CAN TAKE several different forms, and they reach you in different places. The following sections explain the various ways Google+ can let you know about what's happening in your circles and streams.

Email

When you first sign up for Google+, before you've changed any settings (or installed the Google+ app on your smartphone), Google+ notifies you about pretty much everything by email. When something happens on the site that involves you, it sends an email to the address associated with your Google account. For example, when someone mentions you in a post, you'll receive an email like the one here.

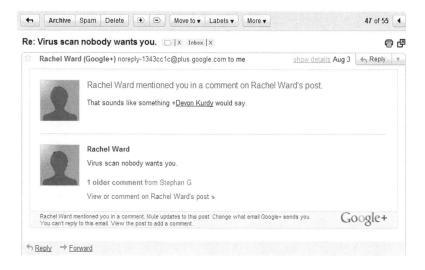

That image shows a notification email in Gmail, but the message should look about the same in Outlook or any other email program. The subject of the email is "Re: Virus scan nobody wants you" because that's the full text of the original post. (Most posts aren't that short, of course, so for longer posts you'd see a truncated version in the subject line, like "Virus scan, nobody wants you, because...") The top part of the email explains what happened—"Rachel Ward mentioned you in a comment on Rachel Ward's post"—and, below that, the mention itself, with the names linked to Google+ profiles. Beneath that is the text of the original post (which may be truncated if it's longer than a sentence or two), a sentence that tells you how many other comments the post had when this email was sent, and a link to the post itself. Below all that, there are a few useful links.

The first link ("Rachel Ward," in this example) goes straight to the profile of the person who mentioned you. The Mute link is really handy, especially if you're getting a lot of emails about this particular post. When you click it, you'll hop straight to your Notifications stream (page 56), where you'll see a notice that that the post has been muted. After you do that, you won't receive any further notifications about activity in that post, and it won't bounce up near the top of any streams even if it starts getting lots of +1s, comments, or edits—just as if you'd manually muted the post in your stream (as explained on page 69).

Click the Change link to open your browser to your Google+ settings page, which is covered in detail starting on page 85. Finally, the "View the post" link opens your browser to the post itself.

These email notifications change in a few subtle ways depending on what you're being notified about. When someone you haven't added to one of your circle adds you to one of theirs, for example, the email looks as shown on the next page.

Jeff Peters added you on Google+   Inbox | x

Google+ noreply-9f03d8ed@plus.google.com to me   show details

Follow and share with Jeff by adding him to a circle.

Don't know this person? You don't have to add them back (they'll only see what's shared with them).
Learn more.

Add to circles

Change what email Google+ sends you. View Jeff's profile or block Jeff completely.

↩ Reply   → Forward

There's a thumbnail pic of the person who added you that links to his profile, a big red button for quickly adding him back, and links to change your notification settings, view the person's profile, and *block* that person to prevent him from seeing anything from you (see page 69).

If someone is already in your circles but they add you to one of *their* circles, the email notification just includes her profile picture, a "View profile" button that links to her profile, and the ever-present Change link.

TIP   If you haven't received any email notifications (you should have gotten one when you joined the site, for example), check your email program's spam folder. Some web-based email services, like Yahoo and Hotmail, can also file notifications in a folder named something like Notifications or Bulk. To make sure your Google+ notifications end up in your main inbox, check your email settings, and click the Not Spam or similar button.

The Notifications Panel

Once you've signed up for Google+, you'll notice that whenever you're logged into your Google account and you view nearly any Google site—such as Google. com, Gmail, Google Calendar, or Google Docs—you'll see a black bar across the very top of the page. (If you've selected a Gmail theme, the bar could be white or gray instead). This is the *Google toolbar*. The left side of this bar contains a series of links to Google services, including, at the far left, a "+[Your Name]" link that takes you to your Google+ Home page. On the right side of the bar, just to the right of your full name, is a small box that's either gray with a 0 inside, or red with a number between one and nine (or "9+" if you're really popular) in it. Click that gray or red box to see a list of your notifications.

NOTE   As this book went to press, Google announced they were changing the Google toolbar, so don't be alarmed if it looks different on your screen than in these pages. To learn about the new design, watch the video here: *http://tinyurl.com/googtoolbar*

A panel drops down, showing your nine most recent Google+ notifications (or fewer, if you haven't received many yet). If you have new notifications, they show up at the top and have a white background, while notifications you've seen before have a bluish-gray background. People's profile pictures are on the left side of the panel, the notification messages are in the middle, and icons indicating the type of notification are on the right: a circle icon means someone added you to a circle, three list-like dots mean the notification relates to a post, and so on. There's a "View all >>" link at the bottom of the panel, which takes you to your Notifications stream. But you know what's even better? Click one of the notifications in the panel.

Devon Kurdy	0	Share...
	Notifications	

Notifications   View all »

Added you (9)   Added you back (1)   ⊚ ›

New photo(s) added from Instant Upload.   ▣ ›

Geeky Sprocket added a comment to a post you commented on.   ≣ ›

Davide Milito sent you a message from CityVille   ♘ ›

Shawn Wilson, Whitson Gordon, and Joseph Rissler commented on a post.   ≣ ›

David Moffitt mentioned you in a comment on a post.   ≣ ›

When you click, the panel changes to display detailed info about whatever it is you're being notified about. Clicking a notification about being added to a circle, for example, displays slightly bigger profile pictures and "Add to circles" buttons so you can click someone's name to view his profile or click the Add button to put him in one of your circles, no matter which Google page you're looking at. (Clicking the Ignore link dismisses that notification so you won't see this person the next time you click this box.) The Newer and Older links at the top-right of the panel let you advance through all your notifications, so you can skip from an added-to-circle one, over to one letting you know you've been tagged in a photo (page 113), and then to one about a +1 on your post. (The "Back to Notifications" link takes you back to the list you saw when you first opened this panel.) Pretty nifty, huh?

TIP When you have the notifications panel open, you can navigate it using the same keyboard shortcuts that work in Google+. Tap J and K to move up and down the list of notifications (a tiny arrow on the left indicates which item you've selected), then hit O (that's the letter o, not the number zero) or your space bar to display the details of that notification (think "O for open"). When you're looking at a notification, J and K work just like the Newer and Older links, respectively, and pressing U brings you back to the main list of notifications.

When you view the details of a notification, the panel includes some reminders of how circles work—noting that you don't have to add people to your circles even if they've put you in theirs, that they'll only see stuff you share with them (meaning your public posts, posts where you specifically mention that person, and posts you share with them), and that people you've already added to your circles can now see items you post to "Your circles" or the circle you placed them in.

But wait, there's more! When you get a notification about a comment or +1, you can interact with the post right in the notifications panel, no matter what Google page you're on. You see the post that got a comment or +1, along with the comment or +1 itself. Click the "# comments" section to see all the comments, or click the number of +1s ("+4," for example) to see who else +1'd the post. You can even comment on the post or mute it—even if just happened to be searching Google or checking your email when you clicked that little red or gray box.

The Notifications Stream

The Notifications stream is similar to the notifications panel, so it should look pretty familiar. You can get to this stream in several different ways. If you're logged into Google+, you can click the Google+ logo, the Home button (its icon looks like a house), or the "+[First Name]" link in the Google toolbar, and then click Notifications in the left-hand list of streams. If you're on some other Google site, open the notifications panel by clicking the red or gray box in your Google toolbar and the click the "View all" link that appears. Phew!

This stream is almost exactly like the notifications, just with a bit more room to maneuver. And just like any other Google+ stream, the Notifications stream will load more items if you scroll all the way to the bottom.

Notifications about posts include a little arrow button in their upper-right corners that's similar to the button that appears in streams (page 69). It lets you report an abusive message, mute a post that's too busy and keeps dominating your stream, or—if it's a notification about a particular post—offer a "Link to this post" that opens the post in its own tab or window so it's easy to copy that post's web address. The More link near the top of the page lets you sort your notifications: Click it and then select an item from the menu that appears to see only circle-related notifications, photo tags, or whatever.

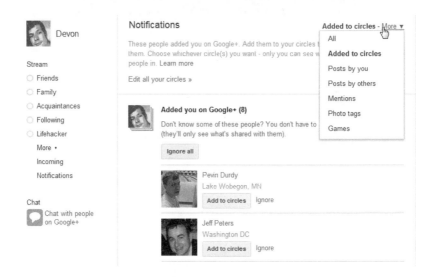

Text Messages

Google+ can send you text-message notifications, but that's a good idea only if you have an unlimited text-messaging plan for your cellphone, and if you're planning to use Google+ only occasionally. As explained on page 87, you can choose to have only very select notifications sent to your phone, but then you may as well just have them sent to your email or, if you have an iPhone or Android cellphone, install the Google+ app (see Chapter 8 for details) and receive the notifications that way instead.

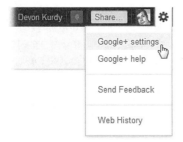

That disclosure aside, if you really did want to have Google+ text you about certain happenings, head to the Google+ settings by clicking the gear icon on the right end of the Google toolbar, and then choosing "Google+ settings" from the drop-down menu.

On the settings page, you'll see a whole bunch of options, which are all covered in the relevant parts of this book. Look for the "Set delivery preferences" header, and click the "Add phone number" link just below it. In the blue box that appears, select your country and enter your cellphone number, then click "Send verification code." After that, check your phone—you should get a text message that reads "Your Google verification code is 123456." Back on your computer, enter that code into the Verification Code field, and then click Confirm.

Set delivery preferences

Email   devonkurdy@█████████

Phone   ▲ Add phone number

Tell us where you want notifications sent to. Your public profile will be discoverable by your phone number.

Country   United States ▾

Mobile Number   +1 7165551234

Verification Code   583212   Confirm

Cancel or Send new verification code

via   ◉ Push notifications   ○ Don't notify me

Now that you've verified your phone number with Google+, you'll see an SMS radio button in the "Set delivery preferences" section of the page. (*SMS* stands for "short message service," and it's just a fancy way to refer to text messaging.) Turn on this radio button to tell Google+ to send all your notifications as text messages. If you've installed the Google+ mobile app for iPhone or Android, you'll also see a "Push notifications" option for sending updates through those apps; Chapter 8 has the details.

There's another option in this section: "Add SMS security PIN." Click this link to add a numerical password to your account. Why would you want to do that? Because with your phone number verified, you can now update Google+ by sending texts to a particular number (33669 in the U.S.). Adding a PIN makes it so that text messages sent to Google+ won't get posted unless the text includes your PIN. That prevents you from accidentally posting a text that you *meant* to send to your significant other ("You looked great after yoga today!"), and prevents your friends from playing practical jokes when you leave your phone unattended.

TIP   Once you've verified your cellphone number, you'll see a "More sharing options" link in the "Set delivery preferences" section of the settings page that you should definitely click. It leads to Google's help page for posting to Google+ by text message, which details some neat tricks. For example, posts you send via SMS are normally shared with "Your circles" (see page 52), but you can share them publicly by adding "+public" at the end of the message, or "+[circle name]" to share with a particular circle.

Below the blue box for setting up your phone is the "Receive notifications" section, which includes a bunch of checkboxes in two columns: Email and Phone (if you've activated SMS notifications as explained above, or have installed the Google+ mobile app). You can turn on the appropriate checkbox to tell Google+ how you want to be notified when someone mentions you in a post, adds you to a circle, tags you in a photo, and so on. Page 85 explains each of these notification settings in detail.

Smartphone Notifications

If you carry around an iPhone, iPod Touch, or any kind of Android phone, you can get updates about what's happening on Google+ contacts right on your device, the same way you'd get a notification about a new email, text message, or whatever.

NOTE The Google+ app works just the same on an iPod Touch as on an iPhone—except that you can't connect to Google+ when you don't have WiFi connection. So wherever this chapter refers to iPhones, the same instructions and tips apply to an iPod Touch.

Android

Once you've installed the Google+ app on your Android phone (see Chapter 8), Google+ notifications show up in the *notification tray* at the very top of your screen (the tray is either gray or black, depending on your version of Android). On an Android tablet, Google+ notifications show up in the lower-right corner of the screen. As with any other Android notification, you can pull down the top tray with your finger to see more details about what Google+ is notifying you about.

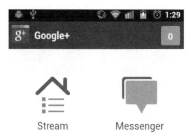

You also see your notifications at the top-right corner of the Google+ app itself. As with the Google toolbar, they appear as a number inside a red square (or 0 inside a gray square, if you don't have any new ones). Tapping or dragging up on this bar displays the same screen you see if you tap the notification in your Android device's topmost notification tray.

The screen that appears is similar to your Notifications stream and notifications panel. It includes a list of recent happenings, an icon next to each one, and a description of what happened. And, like the Notifications stream, you can keep scrolling down to the bottom of the list, and the list will refresh itself, showing you older notifications. Clicking a notification displays the relevant bit of Google+: a post, a list of people who recently added you, and so on.

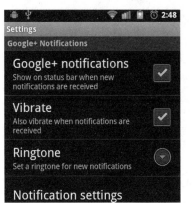

Unlike on the iPhone, you can control your notifications right from the Google+ Android app. While viewing the app's main page or the Notifications list, hit your Android device's Menu button, and then choose Settings from the black tray that pops up. You'll see a list of settings that lets you can choose if and how Google+ gets your attention. You can set the app to vibrate (or not), give Google+ its own ringtone to distinguish it from text messages and other notifications, or turn notifications off entirely.

Tap the "Notification settings" entry, and you'll be taken to a more detailed menu, where you can decide which types of actions you want to be notified about on your phone. Making these changes on your Android phone is the same as making them on the Google+ settings page (page 85), and you'll see them reflected when you next check your Google+ settings.

Notification settings

Posts and mentions

Mentions ☑

Shares ☑

Comments ☑

Comments on a post after I commented ☑

Circles

Adds me ☐

Photos

iPhone

On an iPhone running the latest software (iOS 5, which was released in October 2011), you'll see notifications on the "Slide to unlock" screen that appears when you turn your iPhone on. If you happen to be looking at your phone when a Google+ notification arrives, it appears in a small white bar that drops down from the top of the screen. You can then swipe down on this bar with your finger to bring up the Notifications screen to see, among other things, the latest Google+ activity.

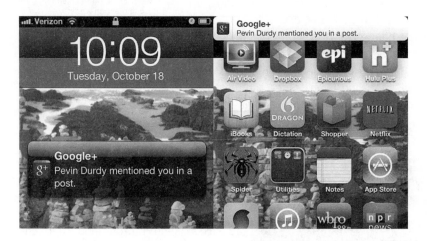

If you're running the slightly older iOS 4 software, you'll get notifications the more traditional (and, to many minds, distracting) way: in a translucent blue pop-up window showing a preview of the notification, with options to View the details or Close the window.

As discussed in the previous section, the settings that control which notifications you receive on your iPhone are on the Google+ settings page, and they're described in detail in the next section. The settings icon on the main screen of the Google+ iPhone app (page 171) doesn't give you any notification options, or even an on/off switch—you have to control notifications from the Web.

NOTE As of this printing, Google+ doesn't have an app specifically designed for the iPad (though this will probably change soon). You *could* install the iPhone app on your iPad, but you probably shouldn't, because it looks funky and isn't easy to use. The notifications do work, but they'll just open in the iPhone-sized app.

Controlling Which Notifications You Receive

GOOGLE+ CAN NOTIFY YOU of just about *everything* that happens on the site that involves you: when people respond to your posts, tag photos with you in them, and so on. But you can also tweak Google+ so it only gives you a tap on the shoulder when something *really* worthwhile happens. This section explains how to tweak the number and frequency of notifications to your liking. You make all these adjustments from the Google+ settings page (to get there, click the gear icon in the upper right of any Google+ page and then choose "Google+ settings").

The Most Important Setting

Not surprisingly, the most important option on the Google+ settings page is the first one: "Who can send you notifications?" This setting is the only way you can control which notifications appear in your Google toolbar and Notifications stream, whereas you can use the settings described starting on page 87 to fine-tune the notifications you get via email and cellphone.

You might not think this setting is all that vital if you only use Google+ to share news with a small group of friends, family members, and acquaintances. They're the only people who can see your posts, so who else could you be notified about?

As you learned Chapter 2, *anyone* can add you to one of their circles, even if you haven't added them to a circle of yours. And anyone you haven't blocked (page 69) can mention you in a post, share a post specifically with you, or tag you in a photo. So unless you adjust this setting, you might get notifications about that annoying guy you only knew in seventh grade when he writes posts about you, uploads embarrassing pictures from your adolescence, and so on. Then again, you might like knowing when people are talking about you and pointing you out in pictures.

To adjust this setting, click the box to the right of "Who can send you notifica-tions?" In the list that appears choose the minimum amount of acquaintance you want to have with the people whose actions result in you receiving a Google+ notification. For example, if you want to know about *every single* mention of you on the site, choose Anyone.

Account overview
Profile and privacy
Google+
Language
Data liberation
Connected accounts

Google+

« Back to Google+

Who can interact with you and your posts

Who can send you notifications? Learn more

Who can start a Messenger conversation with you?

| Anyone |
| Extended circles |
| Your circles |
| Only you |
| Custom |

Set delivery preferences

NOTE You may be wondering about the "Only you" setting—how could Google+ work so that only you can send yourself notifications? Based on experiments and searching, it seems "Only you" is basically equivalent to "Nobody can send me notifications"—in other words, it's a weirdly named Off setting.

If you're using Google+ to interact with particular circles and you rarely (if ever) post items using the Public or Extended Circles options (page 52), it's probably okay to leave this setting as it is (it's automatically set to "Extended circles"; flip to page 55 for a reminder of what that means). If you post things publicly or seem to attract a lot of unknown commenters and sharers who bother you, scale back to Your Circles instead.

If you'd like, you can pick out certain circles and people who can trigger notifications by choosing Custom. In the box that appears, select the circles and people you want using the same techniques you use to select who sees your posts (page 52). When you're done, click Save.

Custom ◆

| Extended circles × | Devon Kurdy × |

+ Add more people

Save   Cancel

NOTE If you've installed the Google+ app on an iPhone or Android device, your Google+ settings page will include a "Who can start a Messenger conversation with you?" setting (shown previously). This relates to the Google+ group-message feature called Messenger; you can get the details on page 183.

The Other Notification Settings

Farther down the Google+ settings page is the "Receive notifications" section, where you can turn checkboxes on or off for each of the things that could trigger a notification.

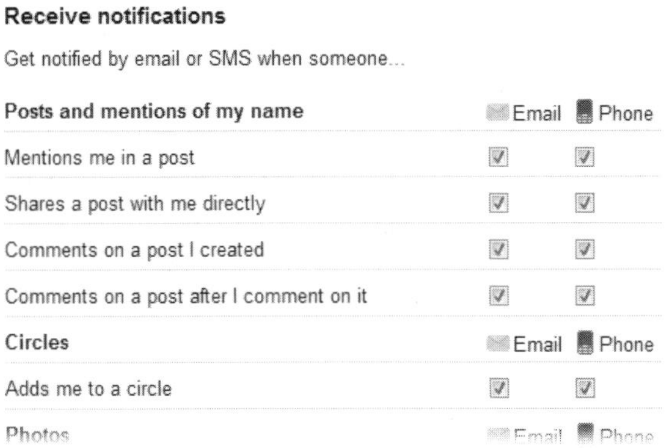

Receive notifications

Get notified by email or SMS when someone...

Posts and mentions of my name	Email	Phone
Mentions me in a post	☑	☑
Shares a post with me directly	☑	☑
Comments on a post I created	☑	☑
Comments on a post after I comment on it	☑	☑
Circles	Email	Phone
Adds me to a circle	☑	☑
Photos	Email	Phone

NOTE If you haven't set up a cellphone to work with Google+ (page 80) or installed the Google+ mobile app, you won't see the Phone column pictured here. If you *have* set up a cellphone to work with Google+, you need to turn on the SMS radio button in the "Set delivery preferences" section of the settings page before you can turn on checkboxes to make Google+ notify you via text message.

The settings are divided into four categories. Here's what each setting means, and a few suggestions on whether to leave them on or turn them off:

- **Posts and mentions of my name.** These control the notifications that get triggered when someone specifically refers to you or responds to your posts or comments:

  - **Mentions me in a post.** As you learned on page 50, people can *mention* you in their posts by adding @ or + signs in front of your name. Only turn this setting off if you get a lot of strangers tagging you.

  - **Shares a post with me directly.** You'll get this kind of notification if someone specifically enters your name in the +Add box (described on page 57) before sharing a post. As with the previous setting, you'll probably want to keep this one turned on unless you're being spammed by more people than you care to block.

  - **Comments on a post I created.** Go ahead and leave this one on, since people can't see your posts unless you share them that way (page 55).

○ **Comments on a post after I comment on it.** This notification setting is perhaps the trickiest. If you leave it turned on, you'll get notifications when someone adds their two cents to a post you left a comment on—but not if you just left a +1. It's safe to turn this setting off if such notifications annoy you, because if people really want you to notice their comments, they can mention you. If just one post you commented on is causing a flood of follow-up comment notifications, you can simply mute that post (page 69).

NOTE If you've set up your cellphone to work with Google+, you can technically turn on the checkboxes in both the Email and Phone columns to receive email *and* text-message or mobile app notifications for each kind of happening, though that's probably excessive for most people.

- **Circles.** You guessed it—this category, which includes only one setting, controls notifications related to circles:

  ○ **Adds me to a circle.** This, more than any other notification, has the highest potential for making you say "Enough, already!" If you keep a low profile online, then you might only see notifications about friends and people you know adding you to their circles, which is fine, since the notification gives you an easy way to add those people to your circles. But if you're getting so many of these types of notifications from strangers that they become distracting, turn this setting off; you can always find out who's added you by heading to your Circles page and clicking the "People who've added you" heading (page 23).

- **Photos.** Since photos can fall anywhere on the spectrum between "worth a thousand words" and "incriminating," you can have Google+ notify you about lots of photo-related actions:

  ○ **Wants to tag me in a photo.** People in your circles can tag you in photos without your permission (though there's a way to change that; see page 115). And folks *outside* your circles can also tag you without permission, though the tags aren't displayed for anyone else who's looking until you approve them. You should almost certainly keep this setting turned on so you know what sorts of photos of you are floating around Google+. (You'll learn all about uploading photos in Chapter 5.)

- ○ **Tags me in a photo.** It's usually fine to keep this setting on because, even though only people in your circles can tag you in photos without your explicit approval, it's nice to see pictures that people post of you.

- ○ **Tags one of my photos.** This is another one you'll want to keep turned on so you can make sure the tagger got the right person and isn't playing a mean joke. (Page 113 explains how to tag other people's photos.)

- ○ **Comments on a photo after I comment on it.** Like the "Comments on a post after I comment on it" setting, these notifications can quickly get annoying if you comment on a popular photo. If someone really wants you to see their comment, they can mention you (page 50), so you can probably turn this setting off.

- ○ **Comments on a photo I am tagged in.** Keep this turned on so you see both the funny *and* snarky responses to photos you're in so you can do damage control, if necessary.

- ○ **Comments on a photo I tagged.** Like the previous setting, you'll probably want to keep this one turned on.

- • **Messenger.** Messenger is a tool available through the Google+ app for cellphones and mobile devices (see Chapter 8). It gives people a way to quickly send notes to each other that's much more convenient (and less awkward) than a chain of reply-all emails. You can read more about how Messenger works in Chapter 8 (page 183). There's only one Messenger-related setting:

  - ○ **Starts a conversation with me.** The Phone checkbox for this setting is turned on automatically, and you can't turn it off because that's how Messenger works: via your cellphone. You'll probably want to keep the Email checkbox for this setting turned on, too, so you don't miss any messages because you don't have your phone handy. If you start getting intrusive Messenger requests from people you don't know, there's a separate setting to limit who can send those; flip to page 186 for details.

> **NOTE** If you've created a Google+ Page for a brand, business, or other organization, you'll also see a fifth category: "Communications about Pages." You can find more info about Pages on this book's Missing CD page at *www.missingmanuals.com/cds*.

Making Notifications Less Intrusive

SO FAR, YOU'VE LEARNED how to control whose actions result in notifications and how to turn on or off most of the notifications you can get by email or on your phone. But some notifications, like the ones you get when people add you to circles, will always show up in your Google+ notifications stream and in the little red box in the Google toolbar described on page 76. And sometimes it just happens to rain activity on Google+, and your inbox, phone, or any web browser open to a Google-related page will keep making noise, vibrating, or displaying new red numbers, again and again. Here's a few tricks you can try to limit the cacophony.

Filtering Email Notifications

Most email programs can filter incoming messages based on who they're from. In desktop email programs like Microsoft Outlook and Apple's Mail, you use *rules* to tell the program to put messages from a certain address into a particular folder. If you use a web-based email system like Gmail, Yahoo Mail, or Hotmail, you can use *filters* to send messages to a certain folder or, in Gmail, assign the message a label. (The exact details of setting up rules or filters depends on your email program; if you have trouble, the program's help files can guide you.)

Using rules or filters, you can keep Google+ notifications out of your inbox, but still keep 'em around so you can check them at your convenience. Google+ notifications all come from different addresses (they start with "noreply-" followed by a string of random numbers and letters), but they all end with "@plus.google. com." So you can set up your email program to filter messages that end with that.

Re: I'm pounding through the Hangouts section...   □   X   Inbox   X

David Drager (Google+)   [image] I'm game, man. View or comme   8:52 PM (13 hours ago)

Chris Van Patten (Google+)   [image] Having never had the opport   9:40 PM (12 hours ago)

Kim Morgan (Google+) noreply-26 show details 1:05 AM (9 hours ago)   ↰ Reply   ▼

Count me in!

View or comment on your po

↰ Reply
→ Forward
Filter messages like this
Print
Add Kim Morgan (Google+) to Contacts list
Delete this message
Report phishing
Show original
Message text garbled?
Mark unread from here
Report Miscategorization

Kim Morgan commented on your post. Mute updates to
Google+ sends you.

You can't reply to this email. View the post to add a c

↰ Reply   → Forward

Keeping the Red Box in Check

Google+ lets you determine exactly which notifications reach your inbox and phone, but if you spend a good part of your day in your web browser, especially on Google-related sites, that little red box in the Google toolbar (page 76), and the way it rolls over when there's a new notification, can be hard to resist.

You can get rid of that distraction (even just temporarily) *if* you use Google Chrome as your browser. (To learn more about Chrome, head to *www.google.com/chrome*.) To do so, install the free "Hide Google+ Notification" add-on from the Chrome Web Store (*https://chrome.google.com/webstore*), and the gray/red box is gone. If you want to get the red box back, head to the main menu in Chrome (click the wrench icon on the right side of the main toolbar), mouse over the Tools menu, and then choose Extensions to disable or uninstall Hide Google+ Notification.

Scaling Back Email and Mobile Notifications

A lot of people leave themselves far too open to distraction on their web-connected phones. As noted above, Google+ gives you different settings to control which notifications you receive on your Android device, iPhone, or by SMS, and which notifications you receive by email. (Those settings don't have any effect on the master list of notifications that shows up in the notifications panel and Notifications stream in your computer's web browser.) Don't configure Google+ so that it sends you every kind of notification about every little thing that happens, or you'll become dulled to all the bulletins and won't notice when something you actually care about happens.

Here are some ways to keep the volume of notifications manageable: Head to the Google+ settings page and set things up so you only get phone notifications about posts where you're mentioned, photos where you're tagged, or posts specifically shared with you. Save notifications about comments and +1s on your posts, comments on posts you've commented on, and other non-direct happenings for email—and, as mentioned earlier (page 90), consider creating a filter so these notifications don't constantly make your inbox look like it has unread messages. Finally, completely turn off notifications for things like "Comments on a photo after I comment on it." You'll still get these notifications in your notifications panel and Notifications stream, unless you've set things so you only get notifications from certain circles (page 85)—and even then, it's probably not vital that you see someone else's comment on your comment, which probably wasn't a deeply thought-out essay.

Now you've got a sense of how to keep in touch and up-to-date on Google+ without having to quit your day job. Next up, you'll learn how to add photos and tag the folks in them so you can give other people a little smile when they check *their* notifications.

CHAPTER 5

Sharing Photos and Videos

HOW EASY IS IT TO SHARE PHOTOS WITH friends and family through Google+? Depending on what you shoot your photos with and where you keep them, the answers range from "easy" to "very easy." Seriously—Google+ makes it super simple to share photos with people, whether or not they use Google+. You get unlimited space to post photos and videos, handy tools to make them look better, and a very slick page for showing them off. If you have an Android phone or use Google's Picasa Web Albums, the photo and video features of Google+ will feel like second nature. If you're an iPhone owner or Flickr fan instead—or even if you've never posted photos before—this chapter will still have you uploading photos in no time.

Just as with posts, you have a lot of control over who gets to see the photos and videos you post on Google+. So you can share snapshots and movies with friends to remind them of all the fun you had at the cabin last weekend—while making sure your boss and mother *don't* see the details of said cabin adventure. This chapter explains how to share your photos with others, view and download the shots other people have shared with you, show off your videos, and organize your photos into albums that are easy for people to see and download.

Viewing Photos

WHEN SOMEONE IN YOUR circles posts a picture and shares it with you, it appears in your stream. But what if you just want to focus on snapshots without all those other, non-photo posts distracting you? As with circles, Google+ includes a page dedicated exclusively to photos. It's your command center for everything photo related. To hop to your Photos page, click the Photos button near the top of any Google+ page

When you arrive at the Photos page, you'll see photos that people in your circles have uploaded. Each photo has a little label on the bottom that indicates who uploaded it ("by Joe Smith"), and if people have commented on a particular photo, it has a small speech-bubble icon in its upper-right corner that indicates the number of comments.

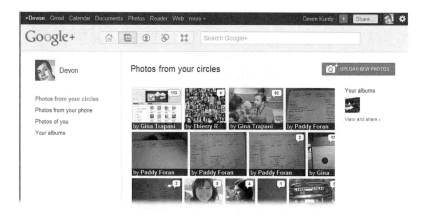

You can change which photos you see in the middle of the page by clicking one of the categories on the left side of the screen, below your profile picture:

- **Photos from your circles.** When you first go to your Photos page, Google+ automatically selects this category (you can tell it's selected here because its name is displayed in red text). When it's selected, your Photos page displays images labeled with the name of the person who shared that photo, and, if anyone has commented on it, a speech-bubble icon.

- **Photos from your phone.** Click the name of this category to see photos you've uploaded from your phone using the Instant Upload feature described on page 107. (As of this writing, Instant Upload is only available on Android phones.)

- **Photos of you.** Here you'll see photos that you've been *tagged* in, either by yourself, by people in your circles, or by people outside your circles whose tags you've approved. (As page 113 explains, tagging is a way to indicate who's in a photo.) If you've been tagged in a photo with another person, those photos also show up in a subcategory labeled "Photos of you with..."

- **Photos from your posts.** These are the photos you've specifically shared with certain people or circles by attaching them to posts or choosing them from among your uploaded albums.

- **Your albums.** This category includes all your photos, even ones you haven't shared with anyone yet. (In Google+, an *album* is a batch of photos you upload in one batch.) You'll also see automatically compiled albums here, like "Photos from posts," "Photos from Messenger" (see page 183), and "Profile photos."

> **NOTE** If you've used Google's Picasa Web Albums service before Google+ to upload and organize photos, you'll see those albums listed on your Google+ Photos page as well.

If you see a photo you're interested in, click it. If it's one of your photos, you'll be taken to a page showing that photo and the other images in the album it came from. Click the photo again and your screen changes drastically: A larger version of the photo appears on a mostly black (or all-black, depending on your browser) background. This distraction-free view is similar to one photographers often use to examine and display their work; Google calls this *lightbox view*.

Near the upper-right corner of the lightbox view screen is an X you can click to get back to the Photos page. The two translucent arrows on either side of the image let you move through the photos. On the right side of the page is a panel where you see, from top to bottom, the person who posted the photo, any comments that have been made about that photo, and a box where you can add your own comment, if you'd like.

Underneath the photo itself are four buttons (or links, depending on your browser): +1 (which indicates how many others have +1'd this photo, if any), Share, "Tag people," and Options. If you're viewing one of your own photos, you'll also see a fifth button or link: Edit Photo; page 119 explains how to use the items in that menu. And at the bottom is a strip of all the photos from this category—in this case, photos shared with you from people in your circles—that you can use as a guide when you're navigating through the images using the translucent arrows.

NOTE
Google+ switches to lightbox view when you click a picture *anywhere* on the site: in your stream, on a profile page, and so on. To return to wherever you were before you hopped to lightbox view, click the X near the upper right of the lightbox page.

Here's the lowdown on each part of this screen:

- **The photo itself.** Clicking it advances you to the next slide, just like clicking the right-facing arrow next to it. Right-clicking it (or tapping with two fingers on a MacBook trackpad) displays a shortcut menu of all the options your web browser gives you for images. Among them will likely be choices similar to "Save image as," which lets you save the image to your computer, and "Open image in new tab" (or "View image"), which opens the image in another browser tab so you can then drag it onto your computer for easier saving.

- **The "John Doe (photos)/Photos from posts" box.** In the upper rightmost corner of the lightbox view screen, you'll see a small profile picture of the person who shared this photo. Clicking on their picture or their name brings you to their profile page. Clicking the "(photos)" link brings you to that person's albums page, which, like your own "Your albums" page, shows all their photos that you're allowed to see. Clicking "Photos from posts" brings you to that section of their photos page, where you see all the photos they've specifically shared, usually with a comment.

- **The comments list.** Commenting on a photo here is the same as commenting on someone's post (page 62). When you add a comment here, it shows up in people's streams just like any other comment.

- **The Share button.** This works just like the Share link in your stream (page 64). Click it to see a pop-up box where you can add a comment and choose which circles or people you want to share it with. Keep reading for a fuller description, just ahead.

- **The "Tag people" button.** This button lets you add tags to photos as explained on page 113.

- **The Options button.** This button displays a few options that differ depending on whether you're viewing one of your contact's photo (and on what restrictions the photo's owner has placed on it, if any) or one of your own photos. If it's someone else's photo, you'll see a "Photo details" option, which displays nitty-gritty info about the shot (aperture, focal length, exposure, and so on). The "Download photo" option does just what it says (you won't see this option if the person who posted the photo specifically turned off photo downloading in their Google+ setting, as explained on page 124). Choose "Report abuse" if the photo is inappropriate, malicious, or otherwise bad for the Google+ community. If you're viewing one of your photos, the Actions menu also includes options for rotating, editing, and deleting the image.

- **The filmstrip at the bottom of the page.** This strip of images (which may not show up if you're viewing one of your own photos that isn't in an album) shows you which photos are included in the particular group you're viewing. For example, the group might include more photos from the person who took the photo you clicked to get to lightbox view. Or if you'd clicked one of the other categories on the Photos page (page 94), the other photos in the filmstrip might be from other people in your circles, from your phone, pictures that you're in, or photos from your albums. Clicking the arrows to the left or right of the picture you're looking at moves back or forward through the pictures in the timeline of photos you're viewing. You can also click any of the little thumbnails at the bottom of the page to bring them up for viewing.

TIP Want to flip through pictures more quickly? You can use the arrow keys on your keyboard to move left and right through a series of pictures in lightbox view. You can also use the J and K keys: J to move forward, K to move backward. (The N and P keys work, too.) Getting familiar with using these keys isn't a bad idea—they move you forward and backward in lots of places in Google+, and in Gmail, Google Calendar, and many other Google services.

Sharing Photos

SHARING PHOTOS IN GOOGLE+ is remarkably easy. The process is slightly different depending on whether you want to share a single photo or a whole album, but either way, it takes just a few seconds.

Head to the Photos page and find the photo or album you want to share. You can share anything you can see on the Photos page, from any section listed on the left: images from your circles, from your phone, ones you've been tagged in ("Photos of you"), and so on.

If you just want to share one photo, that's pretty easy. Navigate to the photo you want to share, and then click it so that it comes up in lightbox view. You should see a Share button (or link) just below the photo. (If you don't, it's because the image is in the "Photos from your circles" collection, and the person who posted this photo "locked" it or specifically disabled further sharing [page 116].) Click this button and you'll get a pop-up box where you can add a comment and choose which people and/or circles can see the image. If you click the tiny arrow circled in the figure, you can disable comments on this post and lock the post to prevent people from sharing it with others. When everything looks good, click Share.

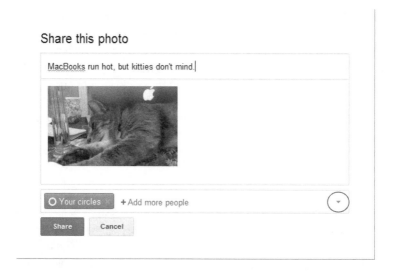

NOTE If you have an Android Phone and you use Instant Upload (page 107), "Photos from your phone," works a bit differently. Clicking a photo in this category just selects it, so you can keep clicking other images to select them, too. To display a photo in this category in lightbox view so you can share it, you have to *double*-click it.

If you want to share an entire album of photos, head to the "Your albums" category, click the album you want to share, and then click the "Share album" button near the top of the page.

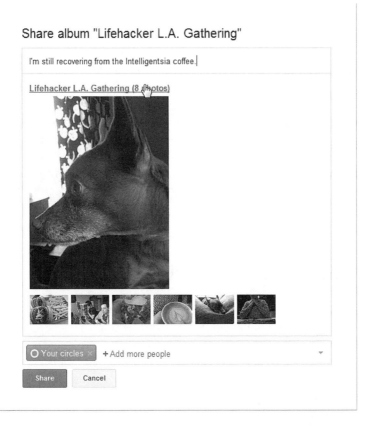

Share album "Lifehacker L.A. Gathering"

I'm still recovering from the Intelligentsia coffee.

Lifehacker L.A. Gathering (8 photos)

So what if you have several different photos you've uploaded to Google+ and want to share, but they're not in an arranged album? Actually, Google+ isn't all that helpful in this case. There's no way to rearrange your albums in Google+ and move photos from one album to another. However, if the photos you want to share are on your computer, you can create a new album by uploading those photos to Google+ in a single batch, either by clicking the Upload New Photos button on the Photos page (page 101), or by creating a new post, clicking the camera icon, and then choosing "Create an album" (page 103). So if you're desperate to get images that are stored only on Google+ into a single album, you could download the images to your computer, and then upload them back onto Google+ so they're all in the same album; it's tedious, but it works. And, remember, you don't need to worry about double-uploading photos, since Google+ gives you unlimited storage space for photos.

Including Photos and Videos in Your Profile

People who've added you to their circles will see your photos in their streams and in the "Photos from your circles" category of their own Photos pages. But you can also share photos and videos on your Profile page so that anyone who seeks you out or clicks your name can see them (assuming you set the images' or clips' visibility to Public, of course).

As you learned in the box on page 15, your profile has a few different tabs, including two labeled Photos and Videos (respectively). Google+ automatically displays these tabs, so you don't actually need to do anything to display them in your profile—they're already there. But if you turned these tabs off while editing your profile, it's super easy to turn them back on. Just head to your Profile page, click the Edit Profile button, and then click the Photos tab and turn on the "Show this tab on your profile" checkbox. Do the same for the Videos tab. (The items underneath these checkboxes—concerning automatic tag approval and geolocation info—are the same as the ones in your Google+ settings, and we'll cover them in just a bit [page 123].)

Getting Photos onto Google+

THERE ARE THREE MAIN ways to add your photos to Google+. You can upload them, either in batches or individually, to Google+ using a web browser. Or, you can upload them from a web-connected cellphone that's running the Google+ mobile app. Finally, if you use Google's photo-sharing service, Picasa Web Albums, you can easily move photos from Picasa over to Google+. The following sections explain all these options.

> **TIP** Flip to page 123 to read about settings that affect all the photos you upload to Google+.

Uploading via Your Browser

It's hard to miss the big, red Upload New Photos button in the upper-right corner of your Photos page.

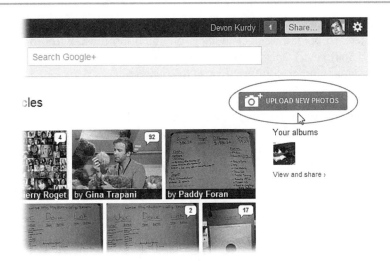

cles

Your albums

View and share ›

When you click it, you see an "Upload and share photos" box that should look familiar if you uploaded a profile picture when you signed up for Google+. What's in the box varies slightly depending on which web browser you use. At the center of the box is a "Select photos from your computer" button. You may also see a message telling you to "Drag photos here" and a dotted line indicating where to drop images you've dragged over from elsewhere on your computer—your Pictures folder, your desktop, or even an attachment in an email program.

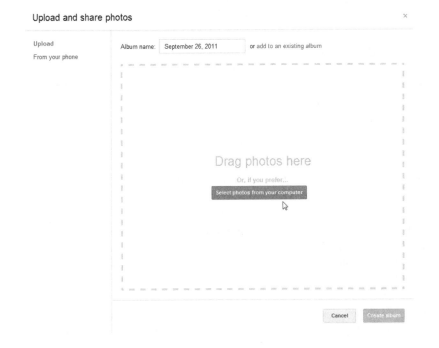

Click "Select photos from your computer" to open a dialog box where you can choose files to upload. (Select multiple photos using the Control [or ⌘ on a Mac] and Shift keys.) Once you've selected the photos you want, click Open (or Choose, depending on your browser) in the dialog box.

Back in the "Upload and share photos" box, Google+ displays a thumbnail preview of each image you dragged over or selected. Move your cursor over or just below a thumbnail and you'll see a few handy icons tools that let you rotate the photo clockwise or counterclockwise or remove the photo from this batch (click the trashcan), and a link you can click to add a caption to the photo—though you'll have time, and much more space, to edit and comment on your photos later, too.

Upload and share photos

If you decide, after seeing the pics you plan to upload, that you want to add a few more, click the "Upload more" link in the lower-left corner of the upload box to re-open the file-picker dialog box. Or, if you saw the "Drag photos here" message mentioned earlier, just drag more photos onto the "Upload and share photos" box.

Once you've selected the photos you want to upload, you can either put them in a new album or add them to an existing one. (In Google+, an *album* is a batch of photos you upload at the same time, although you can add more photos to albums after that, too.) If you're new to Google+ and have never used Picasa Web Albums, you won't have any existing albums to choose from, so use the "Album name" box to give this group of photos a descriptive name, like "Vermont Vacation 2011" or "Fried Turkey Leg Inside a Hamburger Experiment." If you're uploading a bunch of unrelated photos, you could create an album called "Random pictures," or just leave today's date, which Google+ automatically puts in the "Album name" box. To add these photos to an album you created previously, click "add to an existing album" and use the drop-down menu that appears to select the one you want. (You can also do this later, though.)

When everything looks good, click the button in the lower-right corner of the box (if you're creating a new album, it's labeled "Create album"; if you're putting these photos in an existing album, it's labeled "Add photos").

Upload and share photos

The next thing you see is the "Share album" box. Near the top is an "Add a comment" field where you can explain or comment on these pics ("Thanks, Adam, for putting me up in L.A. for a week! Sorry about the avocado stuck to the ceiling fan!"). Just like in a post, you can mention people by adding + or @ in front of their names (see page 50). Near the bottom of the box are sharing controls that let you choose who can see this album. The process is the same as when you're writing a post, as explained on page 52. When you click Share, a notice about your album appears in the streams of everyone you shared it with.

However, you don't *have* to share your photos the moment you post them. If you just wanted to upload these photos to Google+ for safekeeping or you decide you'd rather share them later, simply hit Cancel in the "Share album" box. Your photos still get uploaded to Google+ so they're available to you there, but no one is notified that you posted them.

Uploading as post attachments

You don't have to upload batches of photos to Google+ before you share them. You can simply upload individual photos, or even albums, on the fly as you write a post. Simply start a new post (page 46) and then click the camera icon to see options for uploading photos or albums:

- **Add photos** lets you select a few photos for showing off.

- **Create album** lets you quickly make and name a new album and upload photos for it by dragging-and-dropping or choosing image files.

- **From your phone** (Android only) brings up a pop-up box that shows the most recent photos from your Android phone, if you have Instant Upload turned on (see page 107).

Stream

You'll never believe how much blueberry pie I ate in Maine--until you see it!   ×

Add photos   ×

+ Add photos

⊞ Create an album

▢ From your phone

⊙ Public × + Add more people

Share

If you have an Android phone with the Google+ app installed and the Instant Upload feature turned on, you'll see tiny thumbnails of your most recently uploaded photo right there next to the camera icon, as shown here. Click a thumbnail to select it, and then click more images to select them as well. Once you've selected all the photos you want to attach, click the "Add photos to post" button in the lower-right corner of the pop-up box. You can't get a larger look at these photos from this screen, unfortunately, but you *can* head to your Photos page, select photos in the "From your phone" gallery, and then click Share if you'd like to make sure you're posting the right images.

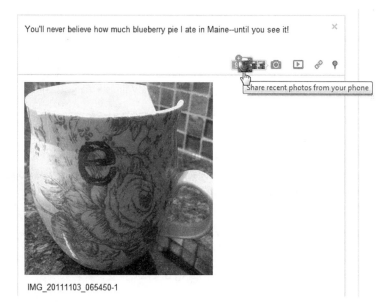

You'll never believe how much blueberry pie I ate in Maine--until you see it!   ×

Share recent photos from your phone

IMG_20111103_065450-1

Uploading from Your Phone

The best camera, the saying goes, is the one you have with you. These days, people carry cellphones with surprisingly decent (and in some cases really *good)* cameras everywhere they go, occasionally snapping pictures of sunsets, cute dogs, delicious meals, and the people they care about. If you have an Android phone, posting photos to Google+ is incredibly simple (even automatic), yet secure. If you have an iPhone, Windows Phone 7, BlackBerry, or any other cellphone that can go online, you can get your snapshots into Google+ with only a modicum more fuss.

NOTE To learn how to install the Google+ app on your phone, flip to page 170. This section focuses exclusively on how to use the app to upload photos, but Chapter 8 explains more about using Google+ on a web-connected phone.

Uploading from an Android phone

If you have an Android cellphone and you've installed the official Google+ app on it, you're always just one snap and two clicks away from shooting and sharing a photo—and sometimes just one click.

After you've installed the Google+ app, agreed to the app's terms of service, and confirmed the Google account you're using with Google+ (see Chapter 8 for details on all these steps), your phone considers Google+ a source for items you want to share, including photos. Go into your phone's Gallery app (sometimes called Photos) and open a photo or select a whole bunch of them.

Tap the Share button at the bottom of the screen. (If you don't see a Share option, you might have to tap the More button first, press the Menu button on the phone itself, or tap and hold the photo to bring up the Share option.) The list of sharing options that appears should include Google+.

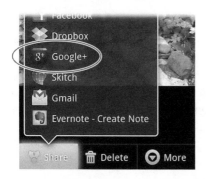

Tap the Google+ menu item to display the screen shown here. Just like when you share anything else on the Google+ website, you get to choose who to share it with, include a location, and add a comment to the photo before you send it out. The layout of this screen is different than the Google+ website, but all the options are there. The circles you're sharing with are shown at the top, in blue, and you can add or modify them by tapping the arrow to their right. Your comment goes in the box below that, and the Post button in the upper right sends the photo to the right peoples' streams.

Create a post

O Family   O Friends

Even at a young age, Zack has his hipster DJ headphone angles down _solid_.

No location attached

TIP Other Android apps that deal in images or photos can Share images with Google+ in this same fashion: Tap the app's Share button, choose Google+, and the photo shows up primed for posting. There's more on sharing photos (and text and links and more) on page 189.

Uploading photos automatically from an Android phone or tablet

The single best feature of the Google+ Android app is its ability to automatically upload photos from your phone to a private Google+ album. Why is that the best feature? Typically, getting all your photos off any cellphone and onto the Web involves hunting down a special USB cable, connecting the phone to your computer, launching a program to sync your photos to your computer, then uploading them through a web browser to a photo-sharing service. And all that is to just get your photos *ready* to share.

The Instant Upload feature on Android phones and tablets makes the upload process much simpler. Once you turn this feature on, it watches your device for new photos and videos. When it finds any, the Google+ app automatically uploads them to a special spot in your Google+ account (and in Picasa Web Albums, as explained in a bit). You might have already seen the "Photos from your phone" category on the left side of your Photos page, and that's exactly where your Instant Upload photos end up. Nobody can see them except you—at least until you choose to share them.

How do you turn on Instant Upload? The most recent version of the Google+ Android app asks you about Instant Upload when you first install the app. If you tell the app to turn this feature on, you then have to decide when you want to upload photos: whenever your phone has a data connection (either *WiFi* [a.k.a. wireless] or *mobile* network [often referred to as 3G or 4G]), or only when you're connected to a WiFi router (usually at home or work). "Over Wi-Fi only" is the safest bet because it can save you from incurring fees for going over your monthly allowance of mobile-network data and prevent battery drain caused by uploading lots of images over a mobile network, which can take forever.

If you disabled Instant Upload when setting up the Google+ app or you want to tweak your WiFi/mobile network preference, you can do that in the app's settings. Head to the app's home page by tapping the gray Google+ logo in the upper-left corner the screen, and then press your phone or tablet's Menu button. (On a phone, this is usually the button just below the screen itself; on an Android tablet, this is the onscreen button in the lower-left corner that looks like a small 3-by-2 grid.) Next, in the row of black buttons that appears at the bottom of your screen, tap Settings. Scroll with your finger toward the bottom of the list of options till you see the Instant Upload section. You can simply check the Instant Upload box to turn it on, but you'll want to tap "Instant Upload settings" to control how your phone sends images over to Google+. More on these settings in Chapter 8.

Uploading from an iPhone

Uploading photos to Google+ from an iPhone is nearly the same as on an Android phone. Assuming you have the Google+ app installed (page 171) and you're signed into your account, open the app and head to the Photos section (page 181). At the top-right corner of the Photos screen, you'll see two icons: a camera and a small stack of what look like Polaroid pictures. Tap the Polaroid icon.

When you do, you'll see a selection screen that you might recognize from other iPhone apps. You can choose from albums you've synced to your phone through iTunes, or select Camera Roll to pick photos taken with your iPhone's camera.

Once you've tapped on a few photos to select them, and then tapped the "Share" button, you'll be given all the options you're used to seeing in Google+ on your computer: a "Share your thoughts" field for adding a comment, a section for choosing the circles and people to share with, and location information you can choose to share (to delete this location info, tap the small X to its left).

At the bottom of the screen are those familiar camera and stack-of-photos buttons. Tap the camera button if you decide to shoot a new photo with your phone, or tap the stack-of-photos icon to pick out a different photo from your gallery. You can also share both a live shot and others from your collection by tapping one icon and then the other before tapping "Post."

Sending photos straight to Google+

It's more convenient to shoot photos with your phone's standard camera app and capture everything you need, and then upload them to Google+ later on using the methods described in the preceding sections. But if you want to share a photo with your friends on Google+ *right away*, you can.

Head to the Photos section of either the Android or iPhone Google+ app and, in the top-right corner of the screen, tap the camera icon. On an Android phone, tapping the camera button brings up a prompt for "Camera photo" or "Choose photo." On an iPhone, the button is separated into a camera for taking live shots,

and a mountain icon for choosing a photo from your Camera Roll. Tap "Camera photo" (Android) or the camera icon (iPhone) and you'll see your phone's familiar camera program.

Once you snap the photo by tapping the shutter button on an Android phone or the camera icon on an iPhone, you can review the shot and tap OK (or Use, on an iPhone) if it's good enough to post to Google+. (Tap Retake to snap another shot, or Cancel on an Android if you decide not to share a photo after all; iPhone folks have to click Retake and *then* Cancel to back out.) After you tap OK (or Use), you see a screen similar to the one shown on page 110 where you can add a comment and choose which circles or people to share with, just as if you'd picked out a photo from your collection.

Pulling Images from Picasa Web Albums

Whether or not you used Google's Picasa Web Albums service before signing up for Google+, by uploading photos to Google+ and sharing them, you're using it now. That's because the services are merged—the photos you upload and share through Google+ are available in Picasa Web Albums, and any photos you might have uploaded previously to Picasa are easily accessible from Google+. You can skip this section if you've never used Picasa Web Albums before signing into Google+, but if you have a stash of photos already in Picasa, this section explains how to share them with your circles.

As noted back on page 8, when you sign up for Google+, Google lets you know that your existing Picasa account will undergo some changes. They're mostly good changes, especially the unlimited storage space you'll receive. Pictures can be uploaded up to 2048 pixels square, and videos, even 1080p HD videos, can run up to 15 minutes in length. And Google+ remembers the visibility settings you originally gave the images on Picasa, so none of your private albums will suddenly go public on you.

Other than more storage space, the main thing that has changed about Picasa are your sharing options. The Picasa site looks the same (aside from a few notices about your new Google+ account), and the photos are laid out the same way. (To get to Picasa Web Albums, go to *www. picasaweb.google.com*.) But click any album and you'll start seeing where Google+ comes in. The fact that the Share button now includes the Google+ icon is one hint.

Now when you want to share an album from Picasa, Google assumes you'll share it through Google+. You'll see the familiar Google+ "Share this album" box, where you can add your comment at the top and choose exactly who to share with.

Share this album

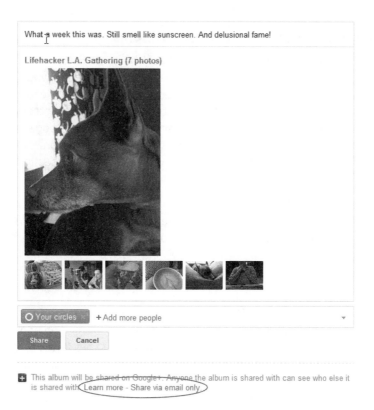

What if you don't want to share an album through Google+, but want to send it out by email invitation instead, the way you used to do with Picasa? You can still do that, but Google doesn't advertise that fact. You'll have to hunt for the small "Share via email only" link at the bottom of the box. Click it to bring up a familiar page for sharing photos by entering email addresses. If you're viewing the contents of an album, you can also click the "Link to this album" link on the right side of the page, and then copy the resulting web address and paste it into an email, IM, or wherever you like.

Individual photos on Picasa Web Albums are still shared through Picasa—either sharing via email or by linking to a photo in an album you've shared or made public. It's a fairly good bet, though, that Google will integrate Picasa into Google+ even more in the future, and that all photos will be available for sharing in Google+, individually or as albums.

Finally, Picasa has its own privacy settings for albums, which you'll want to modify if you set up your account as a place where only you have access to these photos. Head back to your Picasa home page by clicking the "My Photos" tab in the top left of the page (just beneath the black Google toolbar) and then click the "Edit visibility" link on the left side of the page to make changes.

> **TIP** If you've installed the Google+ app on your Android phone and turned on its Instant Upload feature (page 107), you'll see an Instant Upload folder in Picasa Web Albums. This folder contains the same photos as the "Photos from your phone" section of the Google+ Photos page (page 94). Combined with the "Share via email only" link shown on the previous page, it makes the Google+ app a very easy way to share photos from your phone, even with people who aren't on Google+.

Tagging Photos

ONCE YOU'VE POSTED SOME photos on Google+, you can *tag* them to indicate who's in each snapshot. You can even tag other people's photos (if they set the photos' permissions to allow tagging).

What happens when you tag someone in a photo? Just like when you mention someone in a post by adding a + or @ in front of their name (see page 50), they'll see a post, with a link to your photo, in either the stream associated with the circle they put you in or, if you're not in one of their circles, their Incoming stream (page 59). They'll also receive a notification that you've tagged them in a photo, and when they click the notification's link to look at your photo, they'll have the option remove the tag as explained in the box on page 115.

> **NOTE** When you tag someone in a photo, that person gets access to the whole *album* that photo belongs to. So before you tag someone in a snapshot, think about whether the other photos in that album are appropriate for them to see.

To get started tagging, click any photo in Google+, whether it's in your Photos collection or a photo you see in a stream or on a Profile page, to hop to the light-box view with the dark background (you may need to click the photo a second time to get to this view). Under the photo, you'll likely see an "Add tag" button (or link); if you don't, that means the person who posted the photo has disabled tagging, as explained on page 115.

As long as the photo you're looking at has people in it, if you put your cursor over the "Add tag" button (without clicking it), "Click to name" buttons should appear just under each face in the photo. Simply mouse up to the photo and click one of these buttons to add a tag. When you do, a box appears so you can enter the person's name.

Start typing the name of the person in the photo and, just like in a post or a search box, a list of likely candidates appears. If you see the person you're trying to tag, click their name in the list, or tap your keyboard's down arrow to scroll through the list. If you don't find a match, that person probably isn't in your circles, and maybe isn't on Google+ at all. No matter—people don't have to be on Google+ for you to tag them in photos. Just finish typing their name and then hit Enter (Return on a Mac) or Tab; that way you at least have a record of the person's name.

If you don't see a "Click to name" button appear under someone's face when you mouse over the "Add tag" button, that means Google didn't spot that particular face, but you can still tag that person. Just click the "Add tag" button, and a little dotted-line box appears in the photo. It's easy to move and resize this box so that it's over someone's face in the photo. Click and drag within the box to move it, and click and drag the gray circles on its corners to resize it. You just want the box over most of the face, but it doesn't have to be perfect. Then type the person's name in the text box.

If you messed up a tag, or change your mind about tagging somebody, simply move your cursor over their face and look for an X to appear in the upper-right corner of the tag box. Click the X to remove the tag.

Now that you've seen how tagging works, take a peek at your main Photos page again. The "Photos of you" category should make more sense now—it's where photos that you've been tagged in go.

FREQUENTLY ASKED QUESTION

Removing Your Name From Tagged Photos

Somebody tagged me in a photo that I don't want my name associated with. How do I remove the tag?

By default, people that you've added to your circles can tag you in photos, and Google+ will automatically add such tags and make them visible to anyone who can see the photos (and you'll be notified in your Notifications stream). But people who aren't in your circles have to get your approval before Google+ will confirm any photos they've tagged you in so those tags can be searched, and shown to anyone seeing the photo. You can imagine why—someone who doesn't like you could tag you in unflattering photos (or worse).

You can review all the photos that have been tagged with your name by heading to the "Photos of you" section of your Photos page (page 94). Photos in which you've been tagged by people who aren't in any of your circles show up near the top of the page; each one has a checkmark and an X next to it. Click the checkmark to approve the tag, or the X to remove/deny the tag. If you want a better look at the tags and where they're placed, click the photo itself instead. Then you can mouse over where you've been tagged and click the X to remove the tag, just like you can do with tags you've added.

Editing and Deleting Photos

AFTER YOU UPLOAD PHOTOS, you can do a lot with them besides just tag them. In addition to adjusting who gets to see them, you can rotate, delete, and even edit them. And Google+ gives you more than just your standard crop and resizing tools, too—you can nudge slightly off photos closer to perfection, give them an old-timey sepia look, make them black and white, or even make them look like they were shot with a cheap, vintage camera.

> **NOTE** You can only edit photos *you* uploaded, not ones uploaded by anyone else—even if the person tagged you in the photo.

Changing Album Visibility

To change who can see your images, head to the "Your albums" section of the Photos page (page 94). Click an album to see the photos in it, and to share it or change its visibility settings.

Near the top of the page that appears, click the "Share album" button to display a box you've likely seen before. It includes a field where you can comment on the photos you're sharing, and lets you choose which people and circles to share them with.

Click the Options button instead to see a menu that contains just one option (as of this writing, at least): "Delete album." Choosing this option deletes the album *and* deletes any posts about that album.

Underneath those buttons, just above the photos, are the words "Visible to:," followed by a link that reads something like "Only you," "Limited," or "Public." The text of the link tells you who can see your photos when they browse over to your albums, either from your Profile page, or by clicking the "(photos)" link that appears in the upper-right corner of lightbox view when you're looking at someone else's photos. To change who can see this album, click the link ("Only you" or whatever), and you'll have a chance to (you guessed it) add (or remove) circles or people. Changing this setting doesn't actually create a post about this album; it just changes who can see this album if they arrive at your Photos page and look for it.

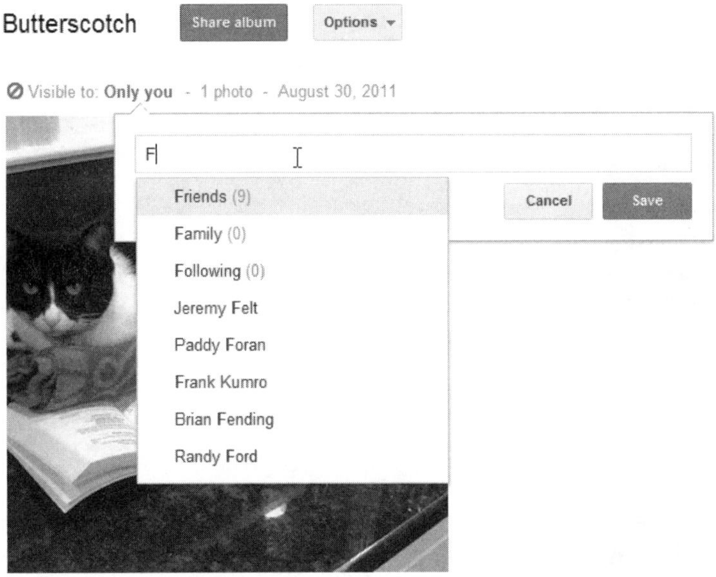

Butterscotch   Share album   Options ▾

⊘ Visible to: **Only you** - 1 photo · August 30, 2011

F| I

| Friends (9) |
| Family (0) |
| Following (0) |
| Jeremy Felt |
| Paddy Foran |
| Frank Kumro |
| Brian Fending |
| Randy Ford |

Cancel   Save

After adjusting the people and circles you'd like to share with, check out the little lock icon below the +Add field. As you learned in Chapter 3 (page 64), people viewing your photos can share them with their own circles, just like they can share posts you write. Click the "Lock this album?" link to get more info about locking albums. Basically, locking an album lets you share its photos specific circles and people, but prevents them from easily sharing those photos with other people. To lock the album, click the box to the left of the lock icon. If you later want to unlock it, simply click that box again. If you want to change a photo back to being visible to "Only you," simply remove all the people and circles from the +Add box, and then turn on the "Lock this album?" box for good measure.

> **NOTE** If you want to do some serious album editing and organizing, it's a lot easier to do that on the Picasa site rather than on Google+. Head to *http://picasaweb.google.com* and click the album you want to edit. Near the top of the screen that appears, click the Organize link. On the next screen, select the photo(s) you want to reorganize (hold down Control [⌘ on a Mac] to select multiple photos). You can then drag them to change their order in the album, or click the Copy, Move, or Delete buttons on the right side of the screen to do one of those things. (If you click Move, you'll see a dialog box that lets you put the image[s] in either a brand-new album or one of your existing ones.) All the changes you make on the Picasa site should instantly be reflected in your Google+ albums.

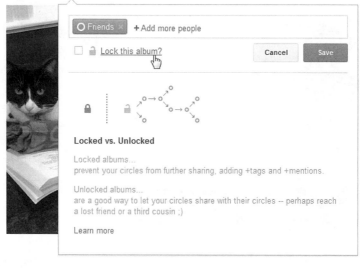

Butterscotch   Share album   Options ▾

♟ Visible to: **Limited** (🔒 Unlocked) - 1 photo - August 30, 2011

○ Friends ×   + Add more people

☐ 🔒 Lock this album?   Cancel   Save

Locked vs. Unlocked

Locked albums...
prevent your circles from further sharing, adding +tags and +mentions.

Unlocked albums...
are a good way to let your circles share with their circles -- perhaps reach a lost friend or a third cousin ;)

Learn more

NOTE   Just like posts, albums you've locked can't be shared by your friends by clicking the Share link at the bottom of your post, but that doesn't prevent your friends from taking a screenshot of your photo, or downloading it through some other geeky trickery. So consider locking more of a request for privacy rather than an iron-clad guarantee of it.

Changing visibility for multiple albums

Above all the photos in the "Your albums" section is a "Change how your albums are shared" link. Click it to display a window with privacy settings for each and every one of your albums. Use the drop-down menu in the middle of each album's row to choose the visibility option you want. Your options are the same ones you learned about back on page 52.

Change how your albums are shared

![photo]	⊘ Finnegan & Butterscotch Photos: 1	Only you ▾	October 23, 2011

                  🌐 Public
                  ⁙ Extended circles
                  ◯ Your circles
                  ⁙ Limited
                  ⊘ Only you

![photo]	⁙ Adorablez Photos: 1		October 13, 2011
![photo]	⊘ Lifehacker L.A. Gathering Photos: 7	Only you ▾	September 26, 2011
![photo]	⊘ Butterscotch Photos: 1	Only you ▾	August 30, 2011

Done

You can change these same settings before you share a batch of photos as an album (page 100) or when you click an album and then click its "Visible to" setting (page 116). But this window is the most convenient way to make changes to a whole bunch of albums or just double-check what people can see when they wander over to your profile and browse through your photos. Once you've got all your albums set the way you want, click Done to close the window.

Changing visibility for individual photos

There is no setting in Google+ to change the visibility of an individual photo. The simplest work-around is to put a photo into its own album, and make that album visible to whomever you'd like, as shown above. Otherwise, Google+ seems to expect that if you have a photo you want to make visible, you'll click the Share button when looking at it in the lightbox view, and send it out to certain people, or whole circles.

Fixing Photos and Getting Creative

Got a photo that could look better, or maybe just looks wrong on Google+? Click it to open it in lightbox view, and then click the Edit Photo button (or link) below the photo to see a menu with a few editing options.

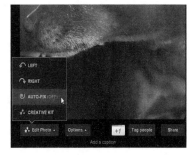

The Left and Right commands pitch your shot 90 degrees counterclockwise or clockwise, respectively. Auto-Fix is just what it sounds like: a tool tries to improve the contrast, lighting, color saturation, and other aspects of your photo. Most often, this tool makes a subtle shift in your photo, which can take a decent photo and make it just a bit better, crisper, or more natural looking. Sometimes, though, Google+ goes a bit overboard, especially with dark, indoor photos taken with a smaller point-and-shoot camera or smartphone. To give Auto-Fix a shot, simply choose it in this menu. If you don't like what it does, simply choose it again to undo the changes.

Choose the Creative Kit menu item and you'll see a new, white box appear—and you'll likely wait a bit, while Google loads its photo-editing tools.

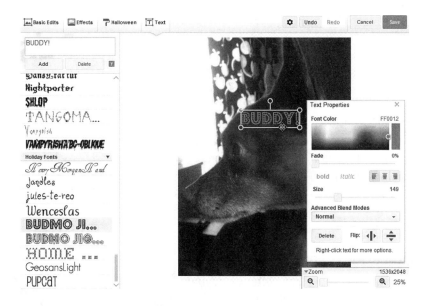

The Creative Kit window is so chock-full of features and looks so much like a separate editing program that it can be kind of intimidating at first. But it only includes a few kinds of tools, with lots of variations on each one. Besides, anything you do to your photo you can easily undo by clicking the Undo button in the window's upper right.

To see the different tools Creative Kit offers, click one of the categories in the window's upper-left corner:

- **Basic Edits.** Along with the Auto-Fix tool you just learned about, you'll find tools here that let you crop, rotate, and resize your image, as well as sliders that adjust exposure, colors, and sharpness.

- **Effects.** Google+ applies these effects to your whole image, giving it a sepia tone, the look of an old camera like the Orton or Holga, a Polaroid-like frame, and so on. Clicking an effect on the left automatically applies it to your photo; move the sliders around, see how it looks, then click either Apply or Cancel to add the effect or remove it.

- **Specialty/Seasonal category.** The exact name of—and offerings in—this category depends on what major holiday is coming up or just passed. For example, as this book was being written, the Creative Kit window included a Halloween category that let you add vampire eyes, blood splatters, and spider webs, among other things.

- **Text.** Select this category and then type some words you'd like to lay over the image in the "Type here…" box at the top left of the window. Next, choose a font from the (fairly substantial) list shown in the figure on page 120, and then click the Add button to place the text on the photo. You then can move the text around and resize it by dragging the little circles on the frame around the word, or click the text itself on the image and drag to move the text. When you click your text, a box pops up with all kinds of settings that let you change the text's color, transparency, size, and even blend mode. Play around and see what works best.

You can undo any effects you apply while messing about in Creative Kit. Even when you click Save in the upper-right corner of the Creative Kit window, you'll get another chance to change your mind: You'll see buttons that let you either replace your original version of the photo with your newly edited version, or save the new version as a copy—highly recommended because, after all, you have unlimited photo-storage space. Choose either Save option and, after seeing some spinning gears and a "Working…" message for a bit, you'll arrive back at lightbox view with your creative new image displayed.

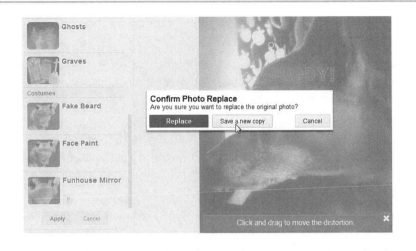

Want even more photo-fixing options? Happily, you don't need to invest in expensive photo-editing software. Google offers two great free options. One is Picnik, which you learned about on page 7; simply head to *www.picnik.com* and upload your photo. The other option is Picasa (*www.google.com/picasa*), a desktop photo-organizing and editing program. Picasa gives you tools for deleting red eye, adjusting lighting, and adding filters, and it has an I'm Feeling Lucky button, which is a lot like Auto-Fix. Most importantly, it lets you easily upload photos to Picasa Web Albums, which (as you learned on page 111) makes it a snap to get those images into Google+.

Deleting and Downloading Photos, and Viewing Details

If you're looking at one of your own photos in lightbox view, the Options menu gives you a few basic controls that are similar to the ones you see when you click Options while viewing other people's Google+ photos (page 96). The "Photo details" and "Download photo" options do the same things as for other people's photos, but there's also a "Delete photo" option and a "Report/Delete comments" option. "Delete photo" removes the photo not only from your collection, but also from any of your posts that it appears in. In fact, if the photo you delete was the only image attached to a post, that whole post gets deleted, too—text and all. So deleting a photo is a pretty drastic move. If you realize you've accidentally shared a photo more widely than you wanted, a better option than deleting it is to restrict who it's shared with, as explained on page 117.

Remember, even if you delete a photo or restrict how it's shared, that doesn't guarantee that it didn't fall into the wrong hands before you did so. Someone could have taken a screenshot of it or downloaded it while it was up. So think carefully before you upload sensitive photos in the first place.

"Report/Delete comments" makes flags and Xs appear on the comments in the box on the right side of lightbox view (if there are any comments). As with a post, you can click the X to remove a comment, or click the flag to report a comment that's really annoying, hurtful, or placed by someone you think has not-so-awesome motives for being on Google+. Reporting a comment brings it to Google's attention, and they can then give the person who posted it a warning—and possibly kick him off the site.

Adjusting Overall Photo Settings

AS YOU'VE LEARNED, MOST of the settings you need to control who can see, comment on, and tag people in photos appear when you click on a photo or album. But you can save yourself some time by tweaking a few options on the Google+ settings page that affect *all* your photos.

To get to the Google+ settings page, head to the upper-right corner of any Google+ page, click the gear icon, and then choose "Google+ settings." (The one place you won't see this icon is in lightbox view, so if you're viewing a photo there, simply click the X to see the gear icon.) On the page that appears, scroll down to the Photos section.

This section contains three settings that affect every photo you post, as well as two links that remind you of how to change which photos and videos people visiting your profile can see. Here's what each option does:

- **Show photo geo location information in newly updated albums and photos.** Most cellphones automatically record your GPS coordinates when you snap a picture. If you turn this setting on and then upload images from your phone, people looking at those photos can click the Options button and choose "Photo details" to see where photo was taken (displayed on a Google Map). If you keep this setting off, you have to manually add location info to a photo (or batch of photos) when you upload them (you can't add location information after that).

- **Allow viewers to download my photos.** It's fine to leave this setting turned on if you don't mind people grabbing copies of your shots. But if you're concerned about your images floating around the Web, or your photos are of a professional or sensitive nature, you'll want to turn this off. Keep in mind, though, that if someone can see your image, there's always a way for them to get a copy of it (by taking a screenshot, for example).

- **People whose tags of you are automatically approved to link to your Profile.** This is where you decide who has the right to tag you in a picture and have that tag automatically approved so that the image shows up in the Photos section of your profile. If you generally like and know everybody you've added to your circles, then leaving this set to "Your circles" is probably fine. But if you've created some circles of people you don't completely trust, change this to just specific circles instead: Family, Friends, and so on.

- The **photos** and **videos** links let you hop directly to the Photos or Videos section of your profile, respectively. Click the photos link to head to the appropriate section, and Google+ automatically puts you in editing mode (as indicated by a red bar across the top of the page) so you can change things like whether any photos show up on your profile, and which photos show up prominently on your Profile page. Click the videos link to tell Google+ whether you want the Videos section included in your profile. When you have things set the way you want, click "Done editing" at the top of the page. (Page 13 has more about editing your profile.)

Sharing Videos

NOW THAT YOU KNOW all about uploading and sharing photos on Google+, working with videos is a piece of cake. You share videos the same way you share photos—you can even share a video on its own or as part of an album.

Uploading Videos

You upload videos to your Google+ account the same way you do photos: upload them directly to the Photos page by clicking the "Upload new photos" button (there isn't a separate button for videos), or as an attachment to a post (page 47). You can also upload a video from your web-connected phone (page 105), or by pulling a video over from Picasa Web Albums (page 111). Anywhere you see a link or button for uploading photos, you can also upload one or more videos simply by choosing a video file instead of an image file.

Google+ can handle the same video formats that work on YouTube: AVI, MOV, MP4, and WMV files, as well as 3GP files from Android and other smartphone cameras and FLV files from Adobe Flash projects. Generally, any video that you can upload to Picasa Web Albums, YouTube, or any another Google service will run just fine in Google+.

TIP If you have an Android phone, the Google+ app's Instant Upload feature works for videos, too. Flip to page 107 for details on setting it up.

Viewing and Editing Videos

Videos are kept in the same place as photos: on your Photos page, under the "Your albums" and "Photos from your posts" categories, as appropriate. They can even be part of an album along with photos. To differentiate videos from photos, Google+ puts a large sideways triangle icon (like a Play button) on videos. When people view one of your videos by clicking on it in a post or on your Profile page, it appears on a black background just like lightbox view for photos. The screen includes playback controls (they're basically a simplified version of the ones you see on YouTube controls), an Actions button, and comment panel.

You can't edit videos in as many ways as you can edit photos. But if you click the Edit button below one of your movies in lightbox view, you can rotate the clip right or left (in case you accidentally held the camera sideways while filming). Click the Options button to see details about it (statistics that are mainly of interest only to A/V geeks), or delete it. The box below explains a few other ways you can edit videos.

Tweaking Videos with YouTube

As noted above, Google+ doesn't give you many options when it comes to editing videos. You can rotate them if they're sideways, but that's about it. Fortunately, you can easily make more elaborate changes by heading over to another site owned by Google: YouTube. Yup, YouTube offers decent, if basic, video-editing tools that are free to use.

–continued–

Head over to YouTube.com and sign in with the same Google Account you use for Google+. At the top of any YouTube page, click the Upload link. If you've never uploaded to YouTube before, you may be prompted to create a username, and a channel name for your videos. On the next page, click "Select files from your computer" button or "Record from webcam" if you feel like doing a little impromptu video performance. After you select a video or record one with your webcam, give it a title, a description, and set its visibility (public or unlisted—either works for Google+). When it's all done uploading, head to *www. youtube.com/editor.* Select the video you want to edit from the thumbnails at the top of the page, and then drag that video down into the empty box below. When you mouse over the video in the lower section, you'll see icons for trimming, rotating, adding effects (which includes fixing lighting and contrast issues), and adding text.

Once you've edited your video, you can attach it to a Google+ post. Simply start a new post as detailed on page 46, click the video icon, choose the YouTube option, and then choose the "Your YouTube videos" heading on the left. If you're signed into Google+ with the same account as your YouTube channel, your edited video should show up there. If not, open a new browser window or tap and pull up your video on YouTube, and then copy its web address; head back to Google+ and paste the address into the "Enter a URL" box.

If you'd like to save a copy of your edited video, you can head to YouTube, click the box in the upper-right corner that has your username and two arrows (like this: >>) pointing downward, and then choose My Videos in the box that appears near the top of the page. On the My Uploaded Videos page, find the video you want to download, then look for a set of buttons underneath it: "Edit info," "Edit video," "Insight," and a downward-pointing arrow. Click the arrow, choose Download MP4, and grab yourself a drink—it will probably take a while. To upload the video to Google+, click the Upload New Photos button on the Photos page, and it'll end up in the "Your albums" section so you can share it any time.

CHAPTER 6

Hanging Out

WRITING POSTS, uploading pictures, and checking out all the things your friends have written and uploaded to Google+ is a great way to let people know what you're up to and keep tabs on what they're doing. But what if you want to connect with people in real time and on a more personal level? That's where Google+ *hangouts* come in. They're a super simple way for you to chat with people using a microphone and (if you have one) a *webcam,* a video camera designed specifically to send video to your computer. (Most newer laptops come with webcams built in.)

In Chapter 3, you learned how your main Google+ stream is kind of like the lobby of a college dorm, and the streams for your individual circles are similar to hallways within that dorm, where everyone's written notes and posted photos on their doors. To continue that analogy, Google+ hangouts are like hanging out in a dorm room with the door open so people can pop in and out. (Or, as Vic Gundotra, Google's Senior Vice President of Engineering put it, hangouts are like sitting on your front porch and letting people know you're there: "Hey, I'm hanging out on my porch. I'm available, [and] if you're available too, you can join [me].") It's a place where you can turn on your microphone and, if you like, your webcam and, well, hang out with your friends. You can see your friends' faces and have meaningful conversations. And best of all, nobody has to install a special program, trade usernames, or "ring" a whole bunch of participants on separate "calls."

You can use hangouts to do whatever you want with up to 10 people: hold business meetings, discuss a document or spreadsheet, or wish somebody a happy birthday in a way that's as close to in-person as possible. The only thing you need to do before using hangouts is to set up some Google+ circles. And at a minimum, you need a microphone that's either built into your computer or plugged into it (although hangouts are more fun if you have a camera, too). This chapter explains the rest.

NOTE Google+ works with most modern web browsers, but you need a pretty fast Internet connection for hangouts to work well. If you're just going to hang out with one other person, Google recommends at least at 900 kilobytes per second (KBps) for both uploads and downloads, though you can squeak by with a bare minimum of 230 KBps uploads and 380–500 KBps downloads. For a hangout with more than two people, Google suggests a download speed of at least 2 *megabytes* per second (mbps) and an upload speed of 900 KBps. Most modern cable and broadband Internet connections should meet at least the two-person requirements, but if you have a really slow connection, you might have to pass on group hangouts until you can upgrade—or you'll end up with frustratingly low-resolution (and possibly choppy) video and stuttering audio.

Not sure of your upload and download speeds? The best way to check is to head to *www.speedtest.net*, and then click the Begin Test button.

Starting a Hangout

IF YOU'VE PEEKED AT the right side of any of your stream pages, you've seen a yellow icon and a button inviting you to "Start a hangout."

Creating a hangout is a lot like writing a post in terms of how you create and share it. You can click the "Start a hangout" button on any stream page, but the simplest thing to do is head to the stream page for the circle that includes the people you want to hang out with and *then* click the button. That way, the people in that circle will see your hangout in their streams. But if it's more convenient, you can click the "Start a hangout" button anywhere it appears and then adjust the hangout's sharing settings later (page 133).

TIP After you click the "Start a hangout" button, you may be prompted to install a *plug-in* for Google's voice- and video-chat services. (A plug-in is a small piece of software that lets your web browser to do a little something extra, like play Flash or Quicktime videos; you probably already have several installed.) You can also download the plug-in from *www.google.com/chat/video*. It's free and works on most modern computers (ones with Windows XP Service Pack 3 or later, Mac OS X 10.5 [a.k.a. Leopard] or later, and most versions of Linux). When you click the Install Plugin button, handy installation instructions appear to help you out. The whole process should take only a few seconds.

Checking Your Setup

After you click "Start a hangout" and your web browser checks to make sure you have the required plug-in installed, a new browser window pops up. The window includes a little motherly advice: check how you look and make sure people can hear you.

In addition to checking your hair and clothes, take a sec to consider whether what's behind you will be too distracting. For example, if you're sitting in a busy café, the other people in your hangout might get annoyed by all the strangers in the background of your video feed, or any screens in sight behind you.

If you're using a laptop with a built-in webcam, Google+ should be able to automatically connect to it and show you what you'll look like to other people in the hangout. If your webcam is separate from your computer, you can plug it in while this setup screen is up; if video from the camera doesn't show up on your screen, try closing the setup screen and then clicking "Start a hangout" again. If that doesn't work, keep reading this section to learn how to troubleshoot it.

The setup screen is small, but it shows what kind of lighting you're got, how your face will be framed when it shows up in the hangout—and whether you need to give your hair a quick finger brushing. Your image will show up much larger when you're actually in the hangout, so try to look your best (or at least presentable).

If you don't have a webcam or are just feeling camera shy, you can still use hangouts. You don't *need* a video connection to hang out—you can just stick to using a microphone. You can also do the opposite—hang out using a camera but no microphone, or a muted microphone—and still hear the audio, but you'd need to type in any comments you wanted to make.

Next, test your microphone. If your computer has one built in, you can use that, or you can connect one to your computer with a USB cable or microphone jack. To make sure it's working, simply say something in a normal voice, like you'd talk to your friends, and watch the volume bars next to the microphone icon at the bottom of the setup screen. If you see at least half of them turn green when you're talking, you're good to go. If only one bar turns green or all the bars do, you're too far away from or too close to your mic.

What if you don't see any green bars at all when you talk, or you don't see yourself in the small window in the middle? Click the Settings button at the bottom of the screen. You'll see a screen where you can test every aspect of your setup: camera, microphone, and speakers. Even if your camera and mic are working fine, it's worth clicking the "play the test sound" link to make sure you'll be able to hear the other people in the hangout, and that your speakers and mic—especially a built-in laptop mic—don't create a nasty feedback loop.

If you're using any equipment that didn't come with your computer—a USB headset or webcam, for example—make sure the proper devices are selected in the Camera, Microphone, and Speakers drop-down menus. Below those menus are two checkboxes you'll probably never turn off. The first one helps prevent echoes, which is nice for everyone listening. The second box gives your computer permission to send reports about your hangout back to Google. It doesn't send anything personal, just notes about how fast your connection is, the frame rate of your video connection, and other geeky numbers that the network engineers at Google would love to have. If you tweaked some settings on this screen to get everything working, click the green Save button. If you don't want to save your changes (or you didn't make any), click the "Cancel changes" link or the X in the upper-right corner of this screen to get back to the setup screen.

Inviting People to Hang Out

Depending on which stream you were viewing when you clicked the "Start a hangout" button, the box on the setup screen below your image will either contain a rectangle representing "Your circles" or a particular circle. If the rectangle represents the group of people you want to hang out with, you're all set—click the green "Hang out" button and flip to the next section.

NOTE   You can *invite* as many people as you want to hang out—like everyone in all your circles—but only 10 people can actually *participate* in a hangout at once.

If you want to hang out with a different circle or with specific people, the process is just like choosing who else gets to see a post or photo (page 52). Start typing the name of a circle or a person in your circles (or even someone who isn't in your circles), and then click or use your arrow keys to choose an item in the list of suggestions that appears.

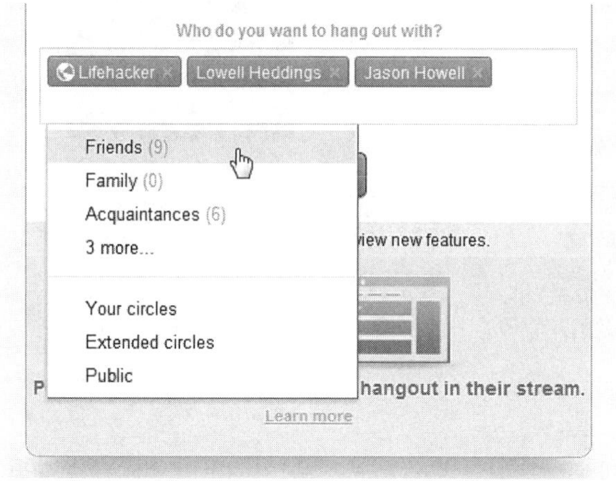

Who do you want to hang out with?

Lifehacker ×   Lowell Heddings ×   Jason Howell ×

Friends (9)
Family (0)
Acquaintances (6)
3 more...

Your circles
Extended circles
Public

view new features.

hangout in their stream.

Learn more

TIP   If the name of a circle or person you *don't* want to invite appears in the +Add box, simply click the faint X on the right side of the rectangle that represents that circle or person.

Inviting someone to hang out means they'll see a notice in their stream that you've started a hangout, and they can click the "Join this hangout" button to join you. (They'll see the "Check your hair" screen before joining, too).

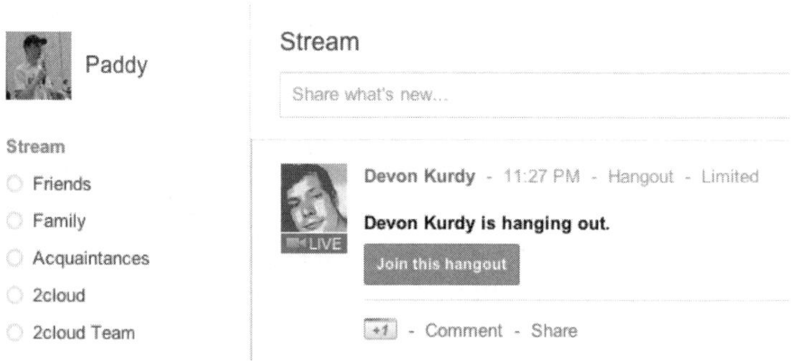

Paddy

Stream

Stream
Friends
Family
Acquaintances
2cloud
2cloud Team

Share what's new...

Devon Kurdy - 11:27 PM - Hangout - Limited
Devon Kurdy is hanging out.

LIVE

Join this hangout

+1 - Comment - Share

If you've invited fewer than 25 people to a hangout (including circles and individuals), then the invitees will also receive a notification that they've been invited to hang out (unless they've changed their settings not to receive them, as explained in Chapter 4). And any Google+ members who happen to be signed into Google Chat when you send out the invite will also see a window with a link to your hangout.

TIP Google Chat, which you can sign into on the left side of your Google+ home page, isn't new or unique to Google+. It's an instant-messaging service that anyone with a Google account can use, and it's included in other Google offerings like Gmail and on Android phones. You can learn more about setting up, signing into, and using Google Chat at *www.bit.ly/gchathelp*.

The people you invite don't have to click Yes or No—they can just ignore your invitation if they don't have time to join you. The whole point of hangouts is that they're semi-spontaneous "Let's chat" invitations, not obligations. Keep that in mind when you're inviting people to hang out—folks with day jobs, for example, might get annoyed if you send repeated hangout pitches during work hours. If someone you've invited to hang out tries to start their *own* hangout while yours is in session, they'll receive a notice that your hangout is already happening so they can consider stopping by yours, instead.

NOTE Just like posts and photos, you can make a hangout public, meaning anyone who finds the invitation in your stream or on your profile page can join in, and they can share the hangout even further when friends of those friends see that they're in a hangout. That can be fun, and perhaps even helpful when you're looking to meet up with a group of strangers, but you'll definitely want to keep reading and learn what to do if things go sour.

Google states on one of its Google+ help pages that "No one owns a hangout," meaning that anybody in the hangout can invite anybody else they'd like to join the hangout. So you may start a hangout with just a few select people, but one of those people could click the Invite button and send an invitation out to all their circles, or even set it as Public, and that invitation will show up in people's streams. The invitation post may include your profile picture (except to people you have blocked) to show that you're one of the participants. So hangouts *aren't* a way to have a *secret* meeting—just like you wouldn't hold a secret meeting on your front porch.

Hanging Out

CAMERA, MICROPHONE, AND SPEAKERS working? Check. Invitations sent? Check. Now that you've done all the prep work, go ahead and click the "Hang out" button on the hangout setup page. When you do, you'll see the following graphic.

Invite more people using the Invite button.

| Invite | Chat | YourExVideo | Mute Mic | Settings | Exit |

Aww. That robot looks so sad with all those balloons and no one to share them with. But no worries—your invitees probably just haven't seen the link to your hangout yet. Remember the dorm room/front porch analogy—folks just need some time to wander by and join in. And hangouts aren't like Skype calls (voice or video calls you make via the Internet), where your chat request "rings" each person individually. Give it some time, and people will start showing up, most likely.

As people start showing up, small versions of their video feeds show up at the bottom of the hangout window, just above the control buttons. (If somebody is going audio-only for this hangout, then you see their Google+ profile picture instead of a video feed.) Google+ tries to figure out who's currently talking and puts that person's video (or picture) in the upper part of the window and makes the image much larger than the tiny ones below. Google+ doesn't do a perfect job of this, but it's pretty good job at switching between speakers. You have to try a hangout or two to get the feel for it, but it's really pretty natural after you settle in.

Down in the lower-right corner of the window are some handy controls. The Mute Video button temporarily turns off your webcam so the other people in the hangout can hear you but not see you (useful, for example, if your toddler niece wanders into the room to show you her new diaper-removing trick). When your video is muted, folks will see your profile picture instead of your video feed. The Mute Mic button turns off your microphone (in case you need to sneeze or answer the phone, say). Click either button a second time to undo its effect, or click the Unmute button that appears at the top of the hangout window. The Settings button takes you to the settings screen you saw on page 133.

TIP When you're in a hangout, it's a really good idea to mute your mic if you need to type something, especially if you're using the built-in microphone on a laptop. The clacking of keys can annoy other participants and make Google+ think you're the one speaking so that it switches the focus of the main video feed from the actual speaker to you, even though you're just looking dead-eyed at a monitor while you type.

The buttons in the lower-left corner of the window are more interesting. Click Invite to bring up the standard circle- or people-picking box so you can type in names of people or circles to invite them to hang out. The Chat button opens up a panel on the left side of the hangout window, where you can type things instead of saying them out loud. This is helpful for pasting in links to websites (or YouTube videos, as explained next), for those hanging out with video but not audio (such as folks joining from work), and when someone wants to contribute a quick thought without interrupting the speaker (especially useful in formal hangouts, like team meetings). Click the Chat button again to collapse the panel.

The YouTube button is mostly just for fun, but it can be a practical tool if there's a video you want to share with the group. When you click the button, the center of the hangout window changes to let you search for YouTube videos. Type a search term in the text field, hit Enter (Return on a Mac), and then click the video you want everyone to see.

After a brief pause while the video loads, everyone will see the video play in the center of the hangout window, so you can laugh, interject, and scratch your chins in real time. You'll also notice that Google+ automatically mutes everyone's mics while the video is playing, then unmutes it when the video ends. That makes some sense, since you're likely soliciting opinions (or just chuckles) from your audience. But if you want to interject something during the video, click and hold the "Push to Talk" button that appears under the video, speak your piece, and then let go of the button.

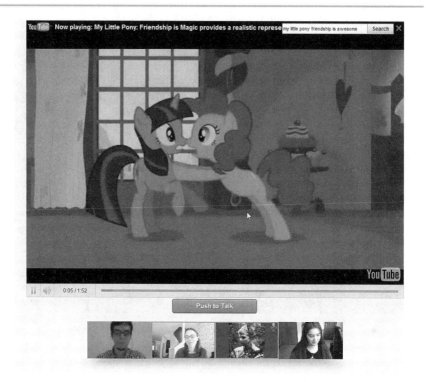

You already know that the Mute Mic button lets you mute your own audio feed. But what if somebody else's audio is causing problems? For example, somebody might step away from their keyboard and not know that their IM program is making a really annoying notification sound. Muting is definitely the way to go for simple annoyances and mic problems. Anyone in a hangout has the power to mute other participants—folks can even mute the hangout's organizer, if they want.

To mute someone, point your cursor at the person's video feed in the row of attendees near the bottom of the window, and you'll see two icons: a green microphone and a red hand. Click the green mic and you'll see a little bar at the top of the hangout window that says "Mute audio for meeting participant [name]?" Click the "Mute now" button to do just that, or Cancel if you change your mind. The person's audio will go quiet so nobody can hear him, and he'll see a quick pop-up notification that he's been muted. It's up to him to unmute himself by clicking the Unmute Mic button in his hangout window. Obviously, muting is more of a temporary fix than a way to solve audio problems. If someone starts muting people just to be annoying, you might want to block them.

The red hand icon is for reporting abuse, which is for more serious problems with a hangout participant. Unlike reporting abuse for posts and photos, though, clicking this icon gives you very specific options for reporting what the person did wrong: they shared adult or violent content, or material that could harm minors; they threatened or harassed someone; they're trying to sell something or they're spamming people; or they're violating copyright laws. If someone is intentionally being a pushy, disrespectful jerk, click the red hand icon below her video feed, turn on the radio button for the type of violation she committed, and then click Report Abuse. (If you want to document the violation, you can take a screenshot of the problem before clicking the red hand icon, and then you can upload that image before clicking Report Abuse.) Google+ moderators will then investigate and might end up booting the troublemaker from the site.

Report a violation of the Google Hangouts Terms of Service.

What happened?

- ○ Adult content
- ○ Harm to minors
- ○ Threats / Harassment
- ● Other Abuse

- ○ Copyright Violation
- ○ Spam / Advertisements
- ○ Violent Content

Optional - Upload a screenshot

[Choose File] No file chosen

Google takes violation claims seriously.

You selected to report abuse of Google's terms of service by Chris Van Patten.

Chris Van Patten

[Report Abuse]   Cancel

NOTE What constitutes a copyright violation? Google doesn't want you to use hangouts to share clips from professionally produced TV shows or movies—no matter how easy it is to find clips from the *Star Wars* online. It's a fine line that Google+ and other social-networking sites are walking, but the point is Google doesn't want you to use the video bandwidth they're giving you and your friends to host film screenings, for example.

When you're done hanging out, click the Exit button in the lower right corner of the hangout window (the X icon), and then close the browser window itself.

One thing worth noting about hangouts is that people you've blocked (see page 69) can't join your hangouts, even if they see that you're hosting one—which they might, if a mutual contact joins your hangout. In that way, hangouts are just like most everything else on Google+: you control who can access your stuff.

Hangouts with Extras

You might have noticed that, on the "Check your hair" screen you see before you start a hangout, there's a "Hangouts with extras" link in the midst of the other buttons and options:

"Hangout with extras" is a good name for what Google+ is offering: the same kind of video chatroom you get in a regular hangout, but with a few interesting doodads to try out. As of this writing, hangouts with extras are just an alternate, still-in-testing version of hangouts, but based on how Google typically rolls out new features, the extras will probably become part of regular hangouts in the near future.

You might choose a hangout with extras if you're organizing a more work-oriented, presentation-type meeting. One of the extras is that you can give such hangouts a name, both so you can make the topic clear (as opposed to the more freewheeling nature of standard hangouts) and so that any documents you create during the hangout can be saved and indexed (more on that in a sec).

To start a hangout with extras, click the standard "Start a hangout" button on the right side of any stream's page. Next, in the window that appears, click the "Hangouts with extras" link shown above, and then click "Try Hangouts with extras." You'll then see a slightly modified "Check your hair" screen where you can name the hangout and choose who to invite. (If you don't name your hangout, Google+ names it after the date and time you started the hangout.) Once you're all set, click "Start hangout."

As you can see in the figure on page 143, the layout of a hangout with extras is a little bit more squared-off and business-like than a standard hangout, but it shouldn't take you long to get the lay of the land.

> **TIP** If you're not sure what one of the buttons at the top of a hangout with extras does, point your cursor at the button to see a little tooltip pop up with the button's name.

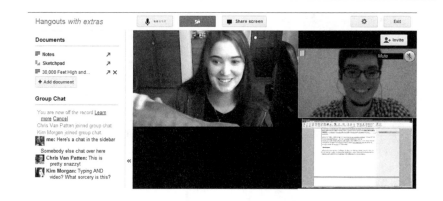

Here's a brief overview of the bonus features you can use when you choose to go "with extras."

Notes, Sketchpad, and Google Docs Collaboration

In the panel on the left side of the hangout window, the Documents section offers three handy tools. Click Notes to display a blank document for, well, note taking. If it'd be easier to explain something by drawing a diagram, click Sketchpad to bring up some simple drawing tools. And if you want to give people in the hangout access to one of your Google Docs documents, click "+Add document." (Google Docs is a site that lets you create word-processing documents, spreadsheets, and more right in your web browser. All you need to use it is a Google account. Check it out at *www.google.com/docs*.)

When you click any of these tools, the document appears in the center of the hangout window, replacing the video of whoever is speaking. Clicking Notes or Sketchpad brings up a blank document or blank drawing pad that everyone in the hangout can see, and which everybody has permission to edit. Whatever people or type or draw is instantly saved to your Google Docs account.

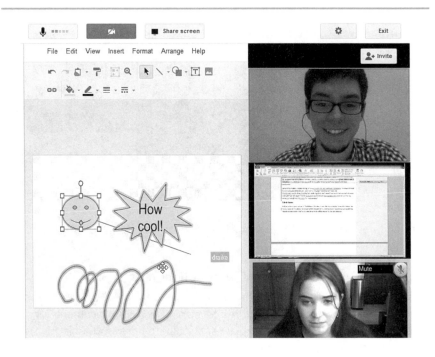

When you're all done typing or drawing, you can head to Google Docs by pointing your web browser to *www.google.com/docs* or clicking the Documents link in the black toolbar at the top of any Google+ page. You'll see the new document or drawing in your list of files. Its name starts with "Sketchpad" or "Notes" followed by "talk.google.com/," and then the name of the hangout in which it was created (if you didn't name the hangout, Google inserts the date and time of the hangout instead).

If you've already created a document in Google Docs that you want to share and work on with your hangout partners, click "+Add document." In the list that appears, turn on the checkbox next to a file's name (you can turn on more than one if you want to share multiple documents), and then click the Select button.

Hangouts *with extras*

Documents

- Notes ⬈
- Sketchpad ⬈
- 30,000 Feet High and... ⬈ ✕
- **+ Add document**

Group Chat

You are now off the record Learn
    more Cancel
Chris Van Patten joined group chat.
Kim Morgan joined group chat.
me: Here's a chat in the sidebar
    Somebody else chat over here

Select a document to share ✕

Google Docs

- Documents
- Presentations
- Spreadsheets
- Drawings

Folders

Upload

Recently selected

🔍

- ☐ 📊 **30,000 Feet Hi...** Oct 14
- ☐ 📊 **Tech News T...** 1:43 PM
- ☐ 📄 **Dec 2011 Fo...** 10:45 AM
- ☐ 📊 **All About Andr...** Oct 16
- ☐ 📊 **Android Guide...** Oct 15

You may see a message asking if you're sure you want to let the people in this hangout collaborate on this document—worth thinking about, because they'll have access to the document *outside* the hangout as well when they log into their own Google Docs accounts, unless you specifically revoke their access by clicking the "Document sharing settings" button in the hangout window, or by heading over to *www.docs.google.com* after the hangout and editing the document's sharing settings. Once you've shared a document, you can switch to a different document by clicking "+Add document" again. Your previous document is added to the Documents list, and you can pull it up again by simply clicking it in the list.

Screen sharing

You've seen how to display documents and sketches in the hangouts with extras window. For anything else you can pull up on your computer, there's screen sharing. To try it out, click the "Share screen" button near the top of the hangouts with extras window.

A window pops up that lets you choose exactly which window you want to share. One of the options is Desktop, which includes *everything* you can see on your screen. Choose either Desktop or a specific window you want to show people, and then click the "Share selected window" button. The window you picked appears in place of your video feed.

If you pick Desktop, things can get a bit tricky, since the folks in the hangout might end up seeing a duplicate of the hangout window, and you have to be conscious of everything you're showing these folks and keep in mind that they can only see a smaller, less clear version of your screen. So it's usually better to share a single window, and use windows and apps with big fonts and large buttons. You can play a video on your shared screen, but it might look really choppy and blurry to the other people in the hangout.

Hangouts on Mobile Devices

IF YOUR ANDROID PHONE or tablet has a front-facing camera (that is, it can take photos of you when you're looking at its screen), and you're running a relatively modern version of the Android operating system, you can take part in Hangouts right through your device—no keyboard or monitor required.

NOTE Google+ Hangouts are due to be available for iPhone and iPad soon, but they weren't as this book went to press. They'll also be available on more Android devices, ones with Android 2.3 and later installed.

To get started, launch the Google+ mobile app (see Chapter 8.) Then simply click the "Join hangout" button in a stream you're checking out, or (if you receive a notification about a hangout) tap the notification. You see the same "Check your hair" screen you get on a computer. Tap the "Hang out" button to join the fun.

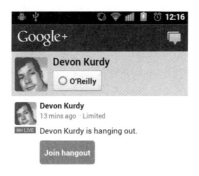

TIP Like hangouts on a computer, mobile Android hangouts require a decent Internet connection: 900 KBps upload and download speeds for two-person hangouts, and 1800 KBps download and 900 KBps upload speeds for multi-person pangouts. You can usually get that with your phone or tablet's WiFi feature turned on and connected to a decent high-speed connection. But if you're on cellular network that's not cutting edge (like some carriers' 3G networks), you might have a rather choppy experience, or not be able to connect at all.

The hangout's main video feed (the one showing the person who's talking) pretty much takes over your device's entire screen. You can check how you look by glancing at the small box in the lower-right corner. The buttons at the bottom let you read and or send chat messages, mute your mic or video, switch to your device's back-side camera, and exit the hangout.

Tips for Better Hangouts

IF YOU'RE GOING TO spare the time—and the computer power—to set up a hangout with a group of friends and acquaintances (and, if you're feeling brave, complete strangers via public hangouts), you may as well do it right. That means having the best possible connection, decent lighting, and the right spirit and etiquette to converse and lead the group along. Some hangouts are meant to be casual and loosely structured, but every hangout can benefit from a little know-how.

Here are a few tips to help you get the most out of your group video chat, drawn from your humble author's experience on live-via-Skype talk shows.

- **Dig out an Ethernet cable.** A wireless connection is okay for most video-chat situations. But to avoid choppiness and get the absolute smoothest video, grab a network cable and connect your laptop or desktop computer directly to one of the outgoing ports on your home router. Video connections suffer a bit from the back-and-forth bounce of a WiFi signal, but a cable connection should give you good video quality as long as you have a fast Internet connection (see the Note on page 130 for the minimum requirements).

- **Grab a USB headset.** You'll get the best possible sound if you use a headset that plugs into a USB port on your computer. The next best thing is to use standard earbud or in-ear headphones (this can help prevent echoes and feedback). If you don't have either of those, go ahead and talk straight at your laptop, but at least determine where your computer's microphone is so you know where to aim. (Finding the mic can be tricky—try Googling your computer's model number or flip through its manual)

TIP Some computers and headsets get angry at one another on occasion, and the result is that you sound like a robot or like you're talking into a spinning fan. If that happens, unplugging the headset and then re-plugging it usually fixes the problem.

- **Speak in full sentences, and wait an extra second before talking.** If you've ever been on a conference call on a glitchy day or made a really long-distance international phone call, you've experience the frustration of talking over the end of someone's sentences, and then apologizing, and then apologizing again for talking over their apology, and so on. That can occasionally happen in hangouts, especially if more than two people have joined. To help avoid that problem, try to speak in full, thought-out sentences with clear conclusions, and occasionally remind others to try the same.

- **Get lots of light behind your camera.** Webcams don't do so hot in low lighting, and your face can end up indistinct if the light is behind your head. Try to set things up so there's an ample light source behind the camera, leaving your face illuminated but not washed out.

The best way to get better at hangouts is to give them a try. Talk to some friends, meet some friends-of-friends, and get used to the idea that you can use Google+'s video-chat service in a way that doesn't feel like an job interview. Line up the camera and get to know the people in your circles.

CHAPTER 7

Searching and Sparks

GOOGLE+ GIVES YOU CIRCLES, streams, and notification tools so you can keep up with your friends, speak your mind, and monitor and control what's going on with your online social life. The site also gives you a way to search out people, topics, and just about anything else that's been shared publicly by someone using Google+, whether you know the people who put it out there or not. Google+ also gives you a personalized stream of news articles and blog posts, dubbed *sparks*, and the ability to make your own news and commentary into potential search results by labeling posts and photos with hashtag markers. This may sound a bit confusing and technical, but it's actually quite simple once you get the hang of it. This chapter will get you up to speed in no time.

Searching Google+

IT'S NO SURPRISE THAT the search bar is a prominent part of every Google+ page (Google made its name as a search engine, after all). The search bar is at the top of every page, with "Search Google+" written inside.

As you know, if you go to Google.com and enter a search term, you'll get results from all over the Internet. The Google+ search bar, on the other hand, scours only Google+. You'll get results that are a mixture of things specific to your Google+ account, and the wider world of things people have posted publicly on the site. Simply click in the box, start typing, and you'll see how that works. You don't even have to hit Enter (Return on a Mac) to see what it finds—even if you just type one letter, Google+ will display a drop-down list with a bunch of suggestions.

Since Google+ is all about connections between people, it guesses that you might be looking for people in your circles, so it puts people in your circles whose names contain the letter you typed near the top of the list. Click any of these folks and you'll arrive at their profile page. This is a much easier way to see what someone has been posting about than heading into your Circles page and finding them there.

Keep typing, and the results change to reflect what you add. Type *great*, for example, and since it's unlikely that any of your friends are named Great, the search results include a host of organizations whose names have "great" in them.

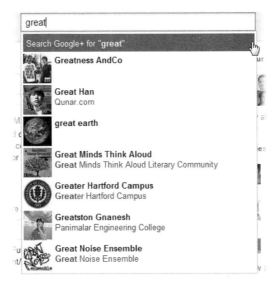

What you're really looking for, though, is great coffee (aren't you always?). Enter that whole phrase, and Google+ runs out of people and organizations whose names match what you've typed, so it provides related search terms instead: "great coffee table books," "great coffee makers," "great coffee coupon," and so on. If one of those phrases if what you want, click it to search Google+ for it.

But you're after plain ol' great coffee: people who've mentioned finding great coffee in a Google+ post, people whose profiles indicate that they love great coffee, maybe even news stories people have shared about great coffee. To search for exactly what you've typed, simply hit Enter (Return on a Mac) or click the first item in the drop-down list (Search Google+ for "[whatever you typed]").

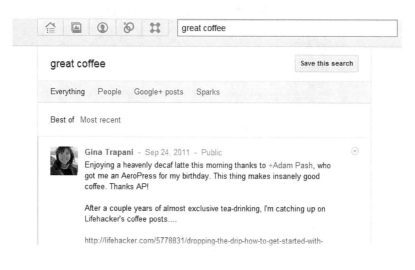

NOTE The search results shown in this chapter will almost certainly look different than the ones you'll get if you search for the same terms because you're connected to different people and will perform the search at different times. Also, search is one of the more rapidly-changing features of Google+.

Google+ brings up your search results, which are tailored to your account. In the "great coffee" search example previously, the top result is a post from Gina Trapani. Why is that? Because she's in one of the searcher's circles, and because of the way the search is filtered. The following sections explain the various filter settings.

NOTE If there are Google+ members who match your search terms, you'll see a small grid of their profile pictures and names at the top of your search results, along with a "View all" link to see more folks who match. For example, do a search for "cheese" and you'll see results that include everyone whose name includes that word, as shown in the following illustration.

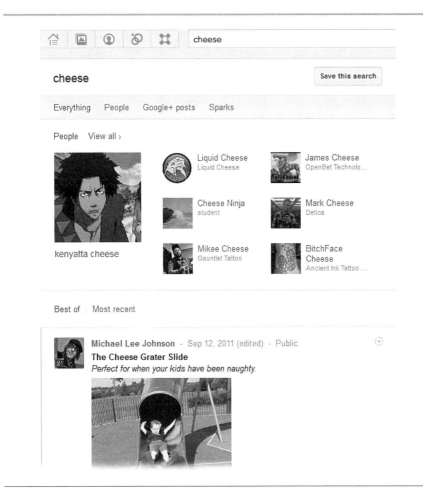

The Four Types of Google+ Search Results

When you perform a Google+ search, the results page that appears gives you a few ways to whittle down your results. In the gray bar below your search term are four categories:

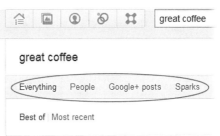

- **Everything.** Google+ selects this category automatically. (You can tell which category is selected because its name is written in gray; the other categories' names are in blue to indicate you can click them to switch to them). When it's selected, the results you see are a compilation of posts, Google+ members, and results from sparks (explained in a sec).

- **People.** Click this category to see a list of people using Google+ who have your search term in their name or profile. You see each person's name, the occupation listed in their profile, a snippet of the first bit of their profile, and an "Add to circles" button you can mouse over to pull up a list of your circles to add this person to. (If the person is already in one or more of your circles, you'll see a button indicating the name of the circle[s] instead.)

- **Google+ posts.** Click this category and you'll see text, photos, videos, and links from people in your circles, as well as from people you don't know who've posted things publicly on Google+.

- **Sparks.** This category is the least straightforward. It displays a kind of curated feed of news and blog items related to your search. The box below has details.

FREQUENTLY ASKED QUESTION

What are Sparks, Exactly?

As a massive, web-wide search company striving for the best results, Google is pretty good at finding news on the Web, particularly breaking news. The Sparks feature (which was a more prominent part of Google+ when the site first launched) is Google's attempt to help you keep tabs on a subject that shows up in the news. Sparks search results come from parts of the Web outside of Google+, so you'll find links to articles, blog posts, and videos about your search term. But Google+ sorts those search results partially by how many times each item has been linked to by members of Google+, and what people are saying about them, which means that relevant and interesting stuff should appear higher up. So sparks are a way to let everyone on Google+ serve as the editors of their own personalized news service.

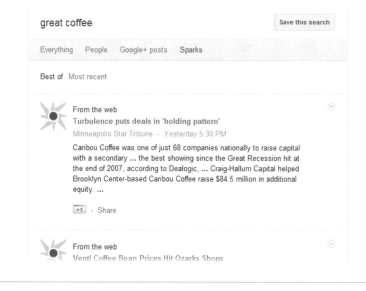

158   CHAPTER 7

Best of vs. Most Recent

Below the four categories described in the previous section, and below any people that Google+ lists at the top of some search results, are two more links you can use to filter your results: "Best of" and "Most recent." Google+ automatically displays search results in "Best of" order. What criteria does Google+ use to rank "Best of" results? They aren't really telling, but it appears that posts are higher up in the "Best of" results for a given topic if they:

- Have lots of comments, +1s, and shares.

- Were written by people in your circles, in your suggested contacts, or in your contact's circles.

- Have all of the terms you're searching for close together. So if you searched for "great coffee," posts that include that exact phrase are ranked higher than posts that simply have "great" and "coffee" separately.

- Have a photo or link attached.

Clicking "Most recent" gives you exactly that—a list of relevant results from the category you selected, with the latest ones on top.

Real-time search results

One thing to note about Google+ search results is that they stay up-to-date, no matter how long ago you searched. The easiest way to see this in action is to click "Most recent." Assuming you search for a relatively active topic (like an upcoming holiday or something related to a breaking news story), you'll see that Google+ is actively checking for newer results. As you watch, the search results page will update automatically, with newer, fresher results appearing at the top of the list.

If you're viewing the "Most recent" results and trying to catch up or want to hold certain stories in place, click the Pause button near the top of the search results. (If you don't see the Pause button right away, it should appear when more results are added to the page.) To go back to automatically seeing the freshest stuff as it comes in, click the same button again, which now reads (you guessed it) Play.

When you have "Best of" selected instead, the updates happen in more methodical fashion. A message appears at the top of your original search results letting you know how many new results Google+ has found since you searched. Click that link, and the page will update to include those items.

Getting Better Results

YOU CAN GET MORE precise search results from Google+ by using *modifiers* to clarify exactly what you're looking for. Here's how to use them to get the most relevant results on Google+.

NOTE The tips in the following sections also work when you're searching the Web using Google.com.

Finding Exact Phrases

Putting multiple words (or one word that has multiple spellings) into quotation marks tells Google+ you want to find that *exact* phrase (or spelling) only, rather than items that happen to include all the words somewhere in them.

For example, search for *monster trucks*, with no quotation marks, and you'll get one set of results. Some of them will likely include the actual phrase "monster trucks," but some will simply contain the words "monster" and "trucks" (like a post that says "The local Ford dealer is having a monster sale on trucks!"). Now search *"monster trucks"*, with quotes, and you'll likely see some different results (though some may be the same). All the results will include that exact phrase, not just the words within it.

Quotation marks also prevent Google from searching for possible synonyms and alternate spellings of your search terms. If you search for *"healthcare"* (with quotes), for instance, your results will only include that exact word and exclude items that mention health care (two words).

Excluding Terms

Certain things are just hard to search out these days. For example, what if you want to see what's happening in Fiji the island nation without having to sort through chatter about Fiji the bottled water brand? Even more difficult: What if you're interested in learning about robots designed to look like humans (androids) but not Google's much-written-about phone operating system (Android)?

That's when you pull out the minus sign (a.k.a. hyphen). Put a minus sign directly in front of a word, with no space, and Google+ won't bring back search results that have that term in them. You can add as many excluded terms as you'd like to narrow things down and get to the results you're looking for.

Say you do a search for *android*. Most of your results will be about the Android operating system. Even if you add *"science fiction"*, with exact-phrase-please quotation marks, you'll still get more stories about phones than robo-people.

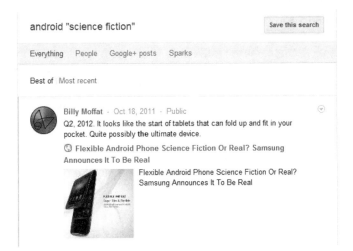

That's when excluding terms comes in handy. To keep techie types and phone obsessives out of your results, add *-phone, -smartphone,* and even *-google* to your search terms. Sure, you might miss a few science fiction-minded items that happen to mention Google searches, but overall, the results are much more precise.

Searching for Multiple Terms

Quotation marks and minus signs help you pare down your results, but sometimes you're feeling expansive. You might, for example, want to see posts about both Korean *and* Vietnamese restaurants in a certain town, rather than having to search them out separately. To do so, type *OR*—in all caps—between two swapable, either/or terms. In the restaurant example, you'd type *"San Francisco" Korean OR Vietnamese restaurant* to see posts about either type of cuisine in the city by the bay. Or say you're craving both cocoa *and* Mexican food; in that case, you might search out *hot chocolate OR tamales*. The first few results might be hot chocolate-related, because it's the more popular item. But scroll down a bit, and you'll see that both chocolate and tamales are represented.

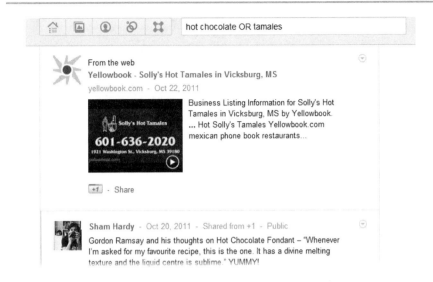

You can combine quotation marks, minus signs, and OR for some super specific results. Searching for *"hot chocolate" OR "dark chocolate" -Ghirardelli*, for example, is one way to really drill down on your high-falutin' sweet tooth.

TIP   You can read more Google search tips by checking out Google's own advice for advanced searching at *http://tinyurl.com/cnl73j*. Not all the tips apply to Google+ (like searching within a website, obviously), but most of them will make you better at finding posts hidden in plain sight.

Saving Searches

SEARCHING GOOGLE+ GIVES YOU the latest and most active posts and news on a topic, but searching out the stuff you're interested in every time you sign into Google+ can be a hassle, especially if you use long, complicated search terms to find exactly what you want. Happily, Google+ lets you save your search phrases by clicking the "Save this search" button in the upper-right corner of every search-result page.

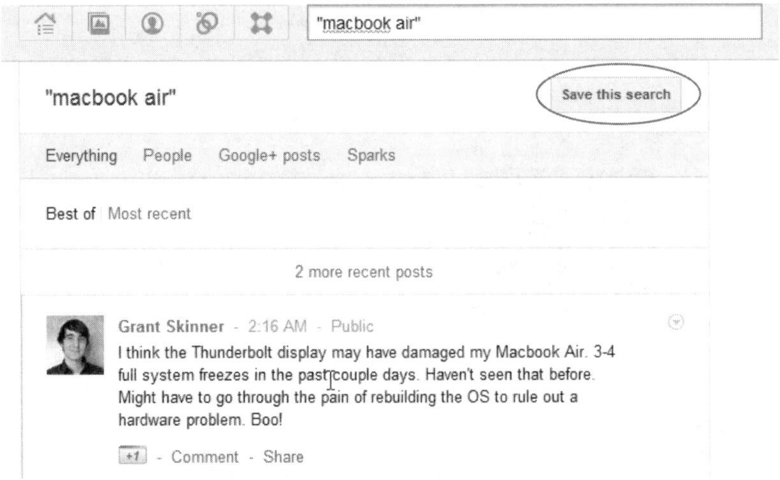

"macbook air"   Save this search

Everything   People   Google+ posts   Sparks

Best of   Most recent

2 more recent posts

Grant Skinner - 2:16 AM - Public
I think the Thunderbolt display may have damaged my Macbook Air. 3-4
full system freezes in the past couple days. Haven't seen that before.
Might have to go through the pain of rebuilding the OS to rule out a
hardware problem. Boo!

+1 - Comment - Share

Whatever you searched for becomes a saved search, which means you can run
a new search on that same phrase by clicking it on the left side of your Home
page, where it appears below the list of your circles. (The little magnifying glass
icon makes it clear that it's a search term, not a circle.) To delete a saved search,
simply mouse over the term, and an X will appear that you can click to delete
the search.

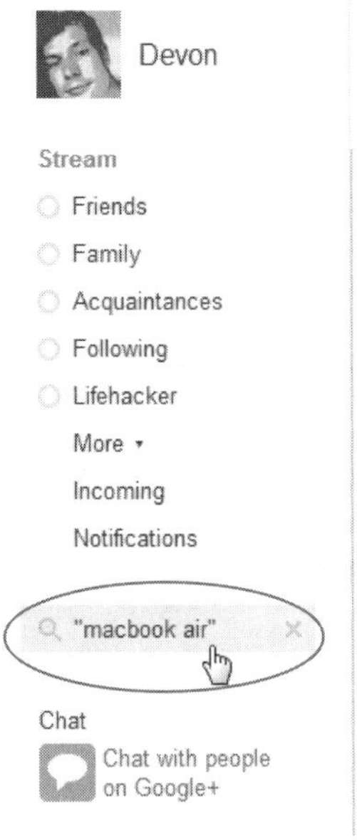

Devon

Stream
○ Friends
○ Family
○ Acquaintances
○ Following
○ Lifehacker
  More ▾
  Incoming
  Notifications

🔍 "macbook air"   ✕

Chat
💬 Chat with people
   on Google+

Note that any of the modifiers you used in your search (like quotation marks) are kept intact in a saved search. And just like with a regular search, you can filter the results to see just people's names, Google+ posts, or sparks, and sort by either the best matches or the most recent stuff.

TIP Google+ makes saving searches convenient, but you can keep more direct tabs on topics in Google+ and access them without needing to have Google+ open in your browser or be signed into your Google account, using either of these browser tricks:

- Bookmark the link for a saved search by clicking the saved search on your Google+ Home page and then dragging it to your bookmark toolbar. Alternately, you can run the search, and then either copy the link in your browser's address bar, or click the + icon at the left end of your browser's address bar and drag the link from the bar onto your desktop or another convenient location.

- Open a saved search in a new browser tab by holding the Ctrl key (the ⌘ key on a Mac) while clicking the search's link, or by right-clicking the search's link and choosing "Open link in new tab" (or something similar). Keep the results fresh by changing the sorting to "Most recent," or by checking in occasionally and clicking the "X more recent post(s)" link.

"What's Hot" Searches and Ripples

Just above your list of saved searches is a "What's hot" link with a little flame icon next to it. Click this link to see the Google+ posts that are currently getting the most +1s, comments, and shares per minute out of all the content on Google+. Most (if not all) of the posts will be by folks you don't know, but you might still find some of them interesting. Running a "What's hot" search isn't terribly useful, but it can be a good way to kill some time. If nothing else, you'll probably see many different kinds of posts that you wouldn't normally see in your stream—for better or for worse.

If you're curious how a post got popular enough to make the "What's Hot" list, click the down arrow in the upper-right corner of the post (circled in the previous illustration), and choose the View Ripples option. This option appears only on public posts that have gained significant popularity. Your own public posts, or posts you share, may even end up with a View Ripples option, if they become popular enough. When you select this option, you'll see a spiffy diagram that shows who shared the post with whom.

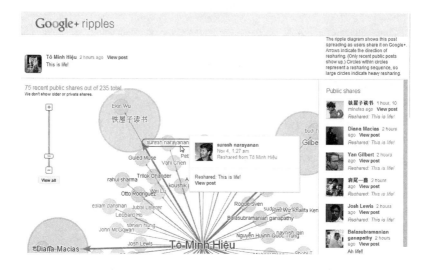

Throw Your Post into the Mix with Hashtags

GOOGLE'S GOOD AT SEARCHING, and as you've seen, Google+ includes some powerful search tools. But you and Google don't have to do all the heavy lifting. In some cases, people will categorize what they post and make it easy to find using a tool that originated on Twitter: *hashtags.*

Hashtags are a word or phrase preceded by the pound sign (#). (In British vernacular and in computer parlance, that symbol is called a "hash.") By adding a # in front of a word (*#SuperBowl*, perhaps, or *#election2012*), Twitter users organize their short updates. Because few people would otherwise write something like "#winning" as part of a message, anybody searching for "#winning" only finds messages where the author intentionally added that hashtag, not every post where someone happened to use the word "winning." So hashtags are a simple way for searchers find messages about a certain topic. They can also give context to otherwise inscrutable posts ("Nice shot Brazil! #worldcup").

Hashtags can even serve as punchlines or indicate that there's some irony at play: "Woke up at 11, ate cereal for lunch, spent afternoon reprogramming remote #Funemployment."

TIP There's no list of "correct" or "approved" hashtags out there—people just make 'em up on the fly. So you don't have to wait to make sure you've seen someone else use a particular hashtag before you add it to one of your posts—you can create them with just a pound sign and a thought. Some catch on and get used by lots of people, others are just one-offs.

The inventor of hashtags, Chris Messina, now works for Google, and hashtags themselves have become a cultural phenomenon. So it makes sense that Google+ has incorporated hashtags into its search abilities. When you or another Google+ member adds a hashtag to a post, the hashtag shows up as a clickable link.

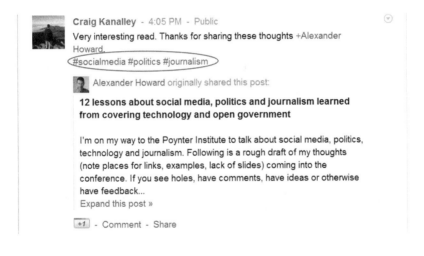

TIP Since Google+ doesn't limit the length of your posts like Twitter does, you can include as many hashtags as you want.

Click a hashtag, and Google+ automatically runs a search for other posts that include that hashtag.

In your search results, you might not see the hashtag itself in the part of the post displayed in the result, but it's in there somewhere—either later in the post (click "Expand this post" to see the rest) or in the comments. And that's the point of adding hashtags: writing about a topic, not worrying about what searchable terms you've used, and then letting your hashtags do the librarian work of categorizing it.

Save this search

Everything   People   Google+ posts   Sparks

Best of   Most recent

Alexander Howard · 4:01 PM · Public

12 lessons about social media, politics and journalism learned from covering technology and open government

I'm on my way to the Poynter Institute to talk about social media, politics, technology and journalism. Following is a rough draft of my thoughts (note places for links, examples, lack of slides) coming into the conference. If you see holes, have comments, have ideas or otherwise have feedback...
Expand this post »

+1 · Comment · Share

As you might imagine, hashtag searches make for great saved searches, because they're more focused and less likely than all but the most specific searches to include unrelated results. They also help you find particular posts. For example, if you knew that John Smith wrote something recently and hashtagged it with "#sabres," you can just search for "John Smith #sabres" to pinpoint John's comments about that (great) hockey team without having to sort through his other posts about hockey.

That's the skinny on searching, sorting, and saving, as well as using and searching for hashtags on Google+. They're all skills you get better at by trying, and it's really hard to harm anything by doing so, so test the limits of what you can find and start adding hashtags to your posts. Next up, a look at how to do almost everything you've learned in your web browser on the smaller screens of mobile devices.

CHAPTER 8

Google+ Mobile

WHAT DO YOU WANT TO SHARE ON GOOGLE+? Chances are, you want to relate things that happen to you, post photos and videos of neat things you see, and link to stuff you find on the Web. A lot of these things come up while you're away from your desktop or laptop computer, but you may have an all-in-one camera, computer, screen, and web connection with you nearly all the time: your web-connected cellphone, or *smartphone*. If you have an Android phone, an iPhone, or most any web-connected device with a decent browser, you can get to your Google+ account from almost anywhere to see what's happening in your streams, add your own two cents (or two pictures), and even add your location to your posts so people nearby can stop in and say hello.

Google+ looks and feels different on a phone or tablet than on a computer, but it should still feel familiar if you're used to working with circles, streams, and sharing tools on your desktop or laptop. In some ways, using Google+ on the go can be a bit more fun—more instant gratification, less thinking through which adjective is just perfect for this phrase. You still have tight control over who you share with and how you get notified of new stuff, but everything gets pared down to the essentials. This chapter explains how to Google+ running on our device and how to make the most of it on smaller screens.

Getting Google+ onto Your Phone

NEARLY ANY CELLPHONE OR device with a good web browser can access Google+ whenever there's an Internet connection available, but Google+ works a good bit better if you install a special program (a.k.a. "app") designed specifically for interacting with Google+ on an Android or Apple device. The following sections explain how to install and configure those apps for the best mobile Google+ experience.

Android Devices

Installing Google+ on most any Android phone is a quick process. Open the Market app on your phone, and then tap the magnifying-glass icon in the upper-right corner. Search for "Google+" or "Google Plus," then choose the app that sports the Google+ icon (probably the top-most option).

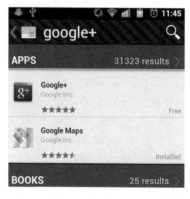

NOTE As of this writing, the Google+ app runs perfectly fine on Android-based *tablets*, too. The tablet app has a few small tweaks to make it a bit more tablet-friendly, it's still basically the same as the phone app, just with more space to work in. The instructions in this chapter are based on the Google+ Android *phone* app, but they work on Android tablets, too.

A potentially easier way to search find and install the Google+ app is to open a browser on your laptop or desktop computer and head to the Android Market (*www.android.com/market*), search for "Google+," and then click the Install button to send the Google+ app over to your phone wirelessly. You'll need to sign into the same Google account your phone is set up to use, but once that's done, you'll have the app on your phone, and have saved yourself some tiny-screen typing.

NOTE On the right side of that Android Market page shown here, there's a small +1 button. If you're logged into your Google account (and you probably are, if you're in the Android Market), you can click this button to give the app a +1 if you've tried it out and have a positive opinion of it. When friends in your circles visit this page, they'll see that you gave this app a +1, so you can serve as a kind of endorsement. The privacy details of these global +1 buttons—ones that appear on sites other than Google+—are covered on page 8; you'll start seeing +1 buttons in more places as Google+ gains popularity.

If you have more than one Google account syncing with your Android device, Google+ will ask you to choose the account you want to use with Google+ when you first launch the app. After that, you'll be asked if and when you want to have photos you take on your phone sent to Google+ automatically via Instant Upload (covered in detail on page 107). After you make your choice, you should arrive at the Google+ Home page.

TIP Want a little more help with your Android device? Check out *The Complete Android Guide*, a front-to-back how-to guide on Android phones and tablets, written by your humble author. You can order printed and ebook versions from *www.completeandroidguide.com*.

iPhone/iPod Touch

Open up the App Store on your iPhone or iPod Touch and search for either "Google+" or "Google Plus." Then tap Free, and then tap Install to, well, install the app.

Alternatively, you can find the app by using iTunes on your Windows or Mac computer. On the left side of the iTunes window, choose the iTunes Store category. Then, type *google+* or *google plus* into the Search Store box in the upper-right corner of iTunes. Look for the result that has the official icon with the "g+" in the middle.

Click the Free button next to the icon, and you'll start downloading the app (you may have to enter your iTunes/App Store password first). With the app installed in iTunes, Google+ should now install itself on your iPhone or iPod Touch if you're running the latest version of the iPhone/iPod operating system (iOS5). If you're running an older version, the app will be installed on your device the next time you plug it into your computer for syncing.

> **TIP** Need a primer on how to grab apps for your iPhone in iTunes or through the App Store? Check out *iPhone: The Missing Manual*, Fifth Edition, by David Pogue (O'Reilly).

After you tap the Google+ icon on your phone or iPod for the first time, you'll be asked to sign into your Google account. Enter the email address connected to your Google account and your password, allow or disallow Google+ to display push notifications (pop-up messages) on your device when you have new notifications (an option you can change at any time in your iPhone or iPod's settings, under Notifications), and you should arrive at the Google+ Home page.

Mobile Web Browser

If your smartphone isn't from Apple and isn't running Android, you're not left out in the cold. On a Windows Phone, a Palm phone running webOS, some newer BlackBerry devices, and most other portable gadgets with a web browser, you can still get into Google+. Simply head to *plus.google.com* in your phone or device's browser.

TIP You can access Google+ via a browser even if you're using an iPhone or Android phone—it works really well in those devices' browsers, in fact. So if you don't want to keep an app installed on your device, or if you want to access Google+ by using a separate Google account from the one the app is tied to, the mobile-browser version is a great option.

At the bottom, you'll see either the email address linked to your Google account or a "Sign in" link. If you need to sign in, tap the link, enter your Google account email address and password, and you'll arrive back at the Google home page.

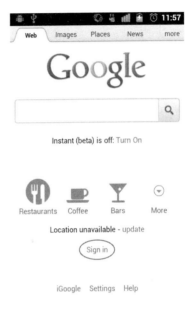

If you happen to be viewing any other Google web page in your mobile browser, there's another easy way to get to Google+: Tap the "more" link in the upper-right corner of the page, and you'll see a whole bunch of shiny icons appear. At the very top is your profile picture, and below that are a few categories. Tap Apps, and then tap the Google+ logo (it's first in line). You may then be asked to give Google permission to access your location and use some storage space on your phone. You should definitely grant it permission to do both so Google+ can work its best. (Google+ will still work if you don't let it use your location, but it won't if you don't grant it permission to use some space.)

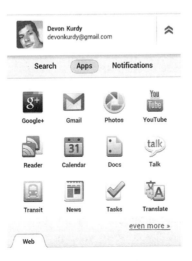

Streams, Posts, and Circles

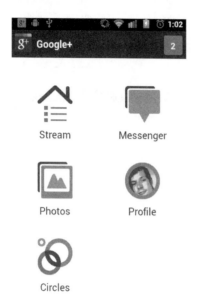

Stream   Messenger

Photos   Profile

Circles

EACH MOBILE VERSION OF Google+ looks and feels a little different, but they're all fairly similar in how you use them. In fact, the Android and iPhone apps are almost exactly alike, except for a few aesthetic differences and some minor details.

If you're using the Android or iPhone app, opening Google+ for the first time brings up a straightforward home page. On Android, it looks like the image to the left of this paragraph.

The home page looks almost identical on an iPhone. All the main sections of Google+ that you see in your computer's web browser—Stream, Photos, Circles, and Profile—get their own icons, and there's also a new Messenger option you'll learn about starting on page 183.

Streams

Tap the Stream icon to check out what's going on with the people in our circles. (On an iPhone, you may see a message asking you to let Google+ use your location, if you haven't already granted that permission. You don't have to allow this, but doing so lets you view the "Nearby" circle described in just a bit.)

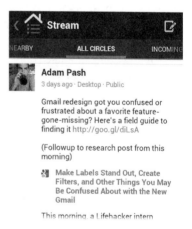

Pretty familiar, no? You see posts from people in your streams, with notes about their visibility, links, images, comments, +1s, and so on.

Near the top of the screen are three headings, which represent streams: Nearby, All Circles (or just Circles), and Incoming. Simply swipe left or right to change streams.

As you'd guess, the All Circles (or Circles) stream shows posts by everyone in all your circles. Nearby is an interesting stream. It includes posts by friends who happen to be geographically close to you, as well as Google+ members you don't know who've written Public posts and shared their locations. (To view this stream, you have to allow the app or your browser to use your location information.) Incoming is the same stream you met back in Chapter 3 (page 59)—it shows posts by folks who've added you to their circles, but you haven't added them back.

How do you view the stream for one of your circles? On an Android phone, press the Menu button, and then choose "Select circles" from the menu that comes up. You'll see a list of your circles with checkboxes that you can turn on to include them in the streams you can thumb through with left and right swipes.

If you're using the iPhone app or accessing Google+ via your phone's browser, you don't have that handy option. Instead, you have to head into the Circles section, tap the Circles tab at the top of the screen, and then tap a circle. Then tap Posts at the bottom of the screen, and you're looking at the stream from that circle.

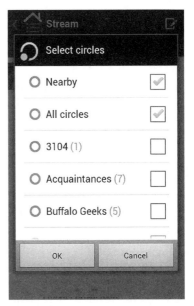

What about all that stuff in the toolbar at the top of the stream page? Exactly what you see there depends on which app you're using.

On an Android phone, the button in the upper-left corner changes to show which section you're in, with a left-pointing arrow at the very edge. Tap the section's icon or the arrow to head back one level—just like tapping your phone's Back button. The pencil-and-pad icon in the upper-right corner is how you create a new post.

The iPhone toolbar is similar. To get back to the home page, tap the square that's divided into smaller squares (the visual cue being, "Here's how you get back to all the

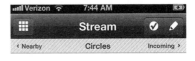

other parts of the app"). Just like on an Android phone, the checkmark lets you *check in* to places (page 178) and the pencil creates a new post. You don't get a camera icon, but you can snap or choose a photo by either going to the Photos section of the app, or by tapping the pencil icon to start a new post and then tapping the camera icon (to take a picture) or the stack-of-photos icon (to share a saved photo). Page 105 in Chapter 5 has the details.

The mobile-browser version of Google+ is almost identical to the iPhone app version, except that you see a Home button instead of the divided square, and you can pull the stream down (drag downwards with your finger) and then let go of it to refresh it.

Writing a Post

To start a post, on the Stream screen, tap the pencil icon. You'll see a blank canvas where you can type your thoughts, add a photo, or share your location.

The Android and iPhone post-writing screens differ a bit, but they're both easy to use. Tap the main blank box to bring up a keyboard so you can type what you want to share, and then type what you want to say. (You might then need to dismiss the keyboard to navigate further—do that by tapping the Back button on an Android phone or the keyboard icon just above the keyboard itself on an iPhone.) Next, tap the + button next to the field that lists the circles you're posting to (on an Android phone) or the text "Your circles" (on an iPhone) to choose who to share with. Tap Done when you have the right circles and people selected. If you'd like to find a specific person to share this post with, tap the magnifying glass icon, start typing his name, and then tap his name when it shows up.

At the bottom of the Android screen where you write posts (shown above) are three icons: a marker (or "pin") that represents your location, a camera, and a stack of photos. If the marker is blue, rather than gray, that means your location is attached to this post; it's listed in the box just below your post text. (You'll learn more about including locations in posts on page 178.) If you're looking to illustrate your post, tap the camera to shoot a photo of something and post it. Tap the stack of photos to choose an image that's already stored on your phone. (See Chapter 5 for more about photos.)

The iPhone app's post-writing screen is similar, just with the photo-adding and location-choosing buttons in different places.

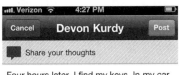

Four hours later, I find my keys. In my car. Eesh.

When your post is ready to share, tap the paper-airplane button in the upper-right corner on an Android phone, or the Post button on an iPhone.

> **TIP** If you get cold feet and decide not to post anything after all: On an Android phone, either tap the Back button or press the Menu button and then choose Discard. On an iPhone, tap Cancel in the upper-left corner.

You can do all the same things via the browser version that you can with the dedicated Android or iPhone app, except for shoot or attach a picture.

In all mobile versions of Google+ apps, links don't get attached to posts the same way they are when you add them to posts in the full browser version of Google+. In the mobile versions, you simply include links in the text of your post, and they'll appear like a normal link in other people's streams.

Including your location (a.k.a. "checking in")

As you learned back in Chapter 3, you can include your location in your posts when you write them on a computer, and the same is true when you write posts from your phone. Google+ refers to this as "checking in," but it's nothing more than adding your location to a post.

If you've tapped the pencil icon to write a regular post, somewhere on the post-writing screen, you'll see a section that either lists your current location or says "No location attached." If you've given Google+ permission to use your location, your location may appear automatically, in which case you don't have to do any-thing to include it in your post. (If you don't want to include your location, you can wipe it out by tapping the X next to it.) To add or change your location, tap the location field on the post-writing screen—a pin-like icon on an Android phone, or the field showing either a location or "Not location attached" on an iPhone or in your mobile browser.

Google+ pulls your location from your phone, compares it to locations it knows on Google Maps, and displays a list of options. The top three choices are your general options:

- **Your current location** is a street-specific description, like Main St, Anytown, Florida.

- **Your city location** lists a more general area, like the name of a town or, if you're in a big city, the name of a district.

- **Hide location** (or "Do not include location") is what you can pick if you change your mind and don't want to include a location. (Selecting this option does the same thing as tapping the X next to the location field on the post-writing screen.)

Below those three options are specific businesses and landmarks that Google found near you. If you're at one of them, tap to select it; if not, use the search box at the top of the screen to try to find the location you want.

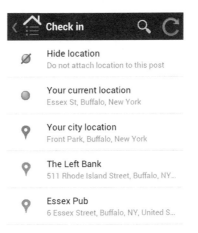

Circles and Profiles

On an Android device, the Circles section is a handy way to view and edit your circles. On an iPhone, or if you're using the mobile-browser version of Google+, the Circles section is the only way to check out an individual circle's stream.

Whichever version you're using, head to the home screen and tap Circles to get started. What you see next depends on how you're accessing Google+, as the following sections explain.

Android phones

The Google+ Android app divides your circles section into two parts, Circles and People. The Circles list shows all the circles you've created, along with the faces of the people in them (if they've signed up for Google+ and uploaded a profile photo). There's a search button in the upper-right corner, which you can tap to search through your contacts, or all of Google+, to find a person. You can tap a circle to see who's in it, press and hold a circle to bring up a "Delete circle" option, or tap the button at bottom to create a new circle.

If you tap the People tab at the top of the Circles page, you see an alphabetical list of everybody in all of your circles. Tap someone's name to jump to their profile page. (At the top of the page, the "Find and invite people" link brings up to the same list of people Google thinks you might know as you'd see in the browser version; see page 24.)

On a profile page, tap the speech-balloon icon in the upper-right corner to start a new *conversation* with the person whose profile you're looking at—basically just a post that's shared only with that person. The tabs at the top of their profile are pretty straight-forward: Posts shows you their most recent posts, About shows their profile info, and Photos displays the person's photos that you have permission to see. On the About page, the gray button to the right of the person's name shows which circles you have them in, and you can tap it to check and add them to (or remove them from) circles.

iPhones and mobile browsers

If you're on an iPhone or using a browser, when you tap the Circles icon on the home page, you may see a list of people's names instead of circles.

Tap the Circles tab at the top to switch to a list of circles. Then tap the name of a circle, and you'll see a list of all the people in it. Tap anyone in that circle to scoot over to the mobile version of their profile page.

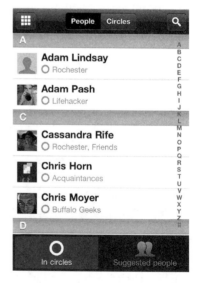

Mobile profile pages are full of stuff you can click:

- **The person's profile picture** to display his other profile photos.

- **The box under the person's name** (which contains the name of one of your circles) to add or change which circles you have him in. (You won't see this button in the mobile-browser version).

- **About** to switch to a view of the person's full profile.

- **Posts** (the default view) to see this person's recent posts

- **Photos** to see pictures this person has posted that you have permission to see.

Viewing Photos

YOU LEARNED HOW TO upload photos to Google+ through a mobile app in Chapter 5 (starting on page 105). Now it's time to learn how to view, share, and manage your Google+ photos on your phone.

> **TIP** As of this writing, viewing photos using the mobile-browser version of Google+ is, shall we say, less than optimal. While some of the basic features work (like swiping to view different images), the controls can be a bit awkward. This version will work, but for a more satisfying photo-viewing experience while on the go, use the Android or iPhone app instead.

From your circles   Photos of you

From your phone   Photos from posts

Head to the Google+ home page, and then tap the Photos icon. You'll arrive at a screen with basically the same options Google+ offers in a full web browser. The Android and iPhone versions of this screen are quite similar, and the browser version is fairly close. The images in this section all show the Android screen, but you should be able to follow along regardless of which version you're using.

The "From your circles" category includes photos posted by people in your circles—in other words, every photo that's been in your stream lately, whether you saw it there or not. "Photos of you" includes all the photos where you've been tagged (page 113), either by yourself or by others. "Your albums" is the personal stash of photos you've uploaded to Google+ (covered in detail in Chapter 5 starting on page 98). And "From your phone" (which you see only in the app versions, not in the browser version) is a handy way of looking at photos stored on your phone, so that you can easily send them to Google+ for sharing.

Tap "From your circles" to check out photos by other people, and tap any photo to view a larger version of it. Tap the photo again to see it alone, without any Google+ buttons around it, on a black background; tilt your phone to rotate the photo for a wider landscape view. Tap the photo again to return to the standard view, with all the buttons and comments. You can tap the tiny "View tags" bar below the photo to see any tags that have been added to it (page 113), and at the bottom of the screen, you can comment on the photo, or scroll down to view others' comments.

To view part of a photo more closely, use the standard pinch and spread gestures to zoom out and in on the photo, respectively. Swipe left and right to see the next photo in this particular group (other photos in this album, from this circle, or whatever).

Uploading Photos

As noted in Chapter 5 (page 105), sharing photos on Google+ from your smartphone is relatively easy—unless you're accessing Google+ via your phone's browser, in which case you should probably hold off on uploading images until you get home to your computer.

To recap Chapter 5 very briefly, here are a few ways to send photos to Google+ for posting and sharing:

- Use Instant Upload (Android only) so that the photos automatically show up in your "From your phone" gallery.

- On an Android phone, tap the Share option on any photo in your photo Gallery or in any other app on your phone that includes photos, and then choose Google+ from the list of sharing options.

- In the Android or iPhone app, tap the camera icon in the upper-right corner while you're in the Photos section of the app, and then shoot, approve, and post a photo.

- Head to the "From your phone" album of the Android or iPhone app, select one or more photos, and then tap the Share button and fill out a post to share with your circles.

Starting a Messenger Session (Apps Only)

HAVE YOU EVER TRIED to coordinate a group of people relatively quickly via text messaging or email to, for example, get everyone to agree on a lunch spot, arrange a time, and give directions? Nobody walks away from such an exchange feeling optimistic about the nature of human communication. Even if you figure out how to send text messages to multiple recipients, the replies arrive without context, and not everybody has access to email on their phone. That's where Messenger, a feature of the Google+ mobile app, comes in. (When Google+ first launched, this feature was called huddles.)

NOTE   While the Google+ mobile website can do a lot of the same tricks as the Android and iPhone apps, you can't use the browser version to start a Messenger session, although you *can* join a Messenger conversation someone else starts.

Tap Messenger on the home page of your Google+ app. There probably isn't much on the page that appears, but Google+ points out just what to do: tap the speech-balloon icon in the upper right to start a Messenger session.

Start a new conversation

Messenger is super-fast group
messaging for your circles. Learn more

In the box at the top of the "New conversation" screen, you can type in people's names or the name of a circle, just like when you share a post. If you're going to be having a prolonged discussion with these folks, it's often smart to create a circle for this purpose (see Chapter 2 for details), but otherwise, go ahead and type in names, and tap to select one of the contacts Google+ suggests.

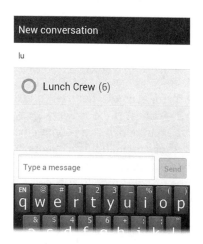

After you select who you want in this Messenger session, type a note in the text box and then tap Send. When you send out your message, what happens next depends on how you're connected to the people you selected. Those who have the Google+ app installed on their phone, have you in their circles, and haven't either blocked you (page 69) or set their notifications to ignore Messenger invitations (page 186) will see your note on their phones right away. Those who don't have you in their circles or who haven't used Messenger yet will be invited to the Messenger session via a notification (see Chapter 4) and they'll see an invite in their streams, too.

TIP To send an image via Messenger, tap the camera icon at the bottom of the screen. You'll get to choose whether to take a new photo or use one that's saved on your phone. Next, either shoot the photo or select the stored one you want to send, and then beam the photo out to your Messenger group. (Images you send via Messenger automatically get added to a special "Photos from Messenger" album in the "Your albums" category of your Photos page; see page 94.)

Even if you head away from the Messenger section of the Google+ app or quit the app entirely, you'll still get notifications about new Messenger messages. The form exact these notifications take depends on your device, the OS it runs, and your Google+ settings.

If you've included people in a Messenger session who aren't on a smartphone with the Google+ app installed, but they're on Google+ and have activated a phone number for text message notifications (page 80), they'll receive an invitation to join your Messenger conversation on their cellphones. If they respond in the affirmative, they'll start receiving texts and be able to reply to the whole group.

You can trade both text and photos in a Messenger session at a pretty rapid pace. And the advantage of this kind of exchange over simply texting or emailing all your friends is that the replies arrive sequentially, and that they're easy to scroll through.

So what happens if you're part of a Messenger conversation where, for example, you've had lunch with the crew and returned to work to attend a meeting—but your Messenger buddies are still going on about a funny thing that happened involving the waiter? To temporarily stop receiving messages from a Messenger conversation (with the goal of perhaps picking them up later and getting back into the conversation), you can mute the exchange. On an Android phone, press and hold the conversation's listing on the main Messenger screen, and then choose Mute. Or, if you're looking at the Messenger exchange you want to mute, tap your phone's Menu button and choose Mute from the menu that pops up. On an iPhone, tap the gear icon in the upper-right of the conversation you want to mute, and then tap the Mute switch to turn it on.

It doesn't harm anything to leave a Messenger conversation open even if nobody's sending anything new, but you might eventually want to formally end the conversation, so you can make room for new Messenger threads. Like muting, you can do this on an Android phone either from the main list of conversations, or from a menu inside the conversation itself. Choose Leave to end the session. On an iPhone, open the conversation, tap the gear icon in the upper-right corner, then choose "Hide conversation."

FREQUENTLY ASKED QUESTION

Restricting Messenger Invites

I've started getting invitations from random people to join their Messenger sessions. Is there a way to stop receiving these invites?

You'll probably only ever use Messenger with your friends, but if you start getting Messenger invitations from folks you don't know or don't want to chat with, you can change your Google+ settings to limit who can send you such invitations. You do this via the Google+ settings page, which you have to access on a desktop or laptop computer, as described on page 85. Look for the "Who can start a Messenger conversation with you?" setting, which is near the top of the page. To scale back from the default setting of Anyone, choose Extended Circles (basically "friends of friends"), or scale down to Circles so that only people in your circles can send you Messenger invites.

Who can interact with you and your posts

Who can send you notifications? Learn more

Anyone ⬍

Who can start a Messenger conversation with you?

Circles ▾

Anyone 🖑

Extended Circles

Circles

Set delivery preferences

Mobile Notifications

THE HOW-TO OF SEEING, responding to, and setting up notification preferences on Google+ for Android or iPhone is covered extensively in Chapter 4 starting on page 82. If you don't have an Android phone or iPhone, you can still see your Google+ notifications on the Google+ mobile website. Simply open your phone's browser, head to the Google+ home page (type *plus.google.com* into the browser's address bar), and then tap the Notifications item.

These notifications look just like the ones you learned about back in Chapter 4. Tap one to see what's happening and why you were informed about it, then tap the Back button in the upper left to get back to the notification list.

Posting to Google+ via Text Message

IF YOU CAN'T INSTALL the Google+ Android or iPhone app or load the mobile-browser version of Google+ on your phone, you can create posts and receive notifications on your phone through simple text messages if you're in the U.S. or India. You learned about setting up Google+ to send you notifications via text message in Chapter 4 (page 80). Once you've got that set-up work out of the way, it's easy to post to Google+ from your phone.

> **NOTE** The directions in this section explain how to create text-message posts if you're in the U.S. If you're in India, you need to send the texts to 9222222222 (really—that's nine 2s, to save you some counting), assuming you're within the +91 country code. Simply swap in that number wherever you see "33669" below.

Create a text message addressed to 33669. (You'll probably want to save 33669 in your contacts under the name "Google+" or "GPlus" so that it's easy to pull up later.) Write out the message you'd like to post. You can include web addresses, which will show up as text links in your post, not as "attached" links with image previews (page 47). If you want to send this post to "Your circles" and you don't have a security code set up for your phone, that's all you need to do—simply send your message and Google+ posts it.

If you do have a security code set up for SMS posting (page 81), you'll need to enter that code somewhere in your text—anywhere is fine, as Google+ will automatically remove it before posting your message. If you want to share your post with a particular circle, type + and then the circle's name, like so: *+foodies.* You can add as many circles as you'd like, but remember that you're limited to 160 characters, minus any security code and your message itself. To post publicly, add "+public" to your post; to share with your extended circles (page 55), add "+extended."

You can share this post with specific Google+ members by adding their first and last names after a +: *How was that mountain bike trip? +devon kurdy.* And if you want to share the post with someone who maybe isn't signed up for Google+, add their email address after a +: *Missing you here in salmon-soaked Alaska! +someone@somewhere.com.*

If you've done everything correctly, you should receive a text back from 33669 that says something like, "Google+ SMS: Your update is successfully posted to your profile."

Google+ treats @ symbols and + symbols the same way, at least when they're sitting right in front of a name or email address. But you'll probably want to stick to the more official + symbol, in case Google+ changes that. Keep that in mind, then, if you're thinking about referring to a Twitter user in a post (Twitter usernames all start with @), since the person's username would disappear and Google would try to share your post to a Google+ user with that name.

Sending Things to Google+ from Other Apps (Android Only)

We've covered how to send photos to Google+ from your phone's gallery, but it's also good to know that the Share button lets you share stuff to Google+ from many other apps on your Android phone. If you come across a neat page in the Browser app, for example, press your phone's Menu button, tap the More option, and then select Share Page. The list that appears includes a Google+ option; tap it to hop over to a post-composing window in the Google+ app, with the link and the web page's title automatically inserted.

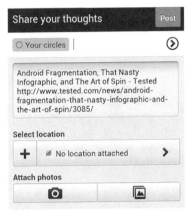

The same thing applies if you find a funny tweet in Twitter, draw an interesting doodle in an art app, or discover a ridiculously good recipe in a culinary app. Most anywhere you can send out text or pictures from your phone, you can usually share with Google+, too.

CHAPTER 9

Playing Games

IT'S FUN TO WRITE DOWN YOUR THOUGHTS; share photos, links, and videos; and comment on others' creations. But sometimes you just want to stack blocks and make them explode, or totally thrash your cousin in a game of Scrabble. The Games page of Google+ is where you can go to get a bit more interactive and competitive with your Google+ contacts. The games are free, easy to set up, and many of them don't require a huge time commitment. You can start a game, play a few rounds on a break, then get back to your offline life. You'll be notified when another player in the game makes their move so you can head back to that game, or any other, at your leisure.

Google+ games are pretty easy to start playing, as they should be, but there are a few tips and tricks that can make them easier to manage, and prevent their notifications from getting annoying. This chapter explains everything you need to know to start gaming on Google+—but you're on your own when it comes to defending yourself against zombies or learning poker strategy.

NOTE Games are the one major part of Google+ that hasn't made it over to the mobile version yet, so you can't get start or join games from either the Android or iPhone app, or the mobile-browser version. That may change, but for now, you can only play Google+ games in a computer's web browser.

Getting into Games

YOU CAN GET TO the Games page right from the gray taskbar near the top of every Google+ page.

You can also get to the Games page by clicking a notification from another Google+ member who asks you to join in a game, check out their accomplishment, or somehow help them in a game. You'll see these notifications in the usual spots: in the black Google toolbar, in your notifications stream, and possibly on your phone. (See Chapter 4 for more about notifications). If you remember receiving such a notification but you can't find it now, head to the Notifications section of your main Stream page, click the More link to the upper-right of the notifications shown in the center, and then choose Games.

> **TIP** Another way to view your game-related notifications: Head to the Games page and then click "Game notifications" on the left side of the screen.

To quickly join a game you've been invited to or notified about, click the "Play now" link in the message or post.

Starting a Game

WHEN YOU ARRIVE AT the Games page, you'll notice it's quite a bit different from the other areas of Google+. In the center of the screen is a constantly changing section promoting "featured" games (whatever that means). If one of these games looks interesting, click the Play button in the lower-left of this section. You can check out other featured games by clicking their thumbnails in the lower right of the big promo box.

The Games stream section, farther down the page, shows all the recent activity by your friends who are sharing Google+ game achievements. Google+ intentionally tucks these little posts about achievements and requests for help from friends into this section of the Games page so you can ignore them in your main stream and see them collected here whenever you feel like checking on what's happening in Procrastination Central. They're not the same as direct notifications sent your way—those are handled in the Notifications stream.

Games stream

Devon Kurdy · 2:14 PM · Game Update · Limited

Triple Town - I built a Outpost in Triple Town!
Devon Kurdy earned 30,650 points in 209 years. Can you do better?

Triple Town, by Spry Fox, is an original puzzle game in which you try to create a great city!

+1 · Comment · Share

Scott Leffler · Oct 5, 2011 · Game Update · Public

Bejeweled Blitz - I brought the bling and earned this 175k Star Medal in Bejeweled Blitz.
Scott is going to need sunglasses because of all their glittering Star Medals! Want your own Star Medals? Then come play!

Join My Team!

Just like on the Stream page, you can use the links on the left side of the Games page to change what you're looking at. When you arrive, you see the "Featured games" section. To see all the games Google+ has to offer, click the "All games" link (clicking "More games" below the promo box does the same thing). As of this writing, there are a total of 21 games, but that number is sure to rise.

All games

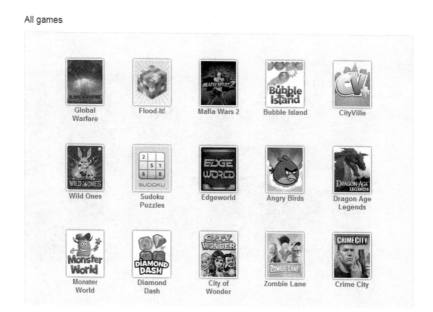

The "All games" screen doesn't provide much information about the games, though you can infer a few things from the games' icons and names (Crime City, for example, doesn't look like a game for pacifists). Click any game to get a better sense of what it's about.

The first time you play a Google+ game, though, Google+ displays a box let you know that games are "social." In other words, other people on Google+ will be able to see that you're playing. For example, when people who've put you in their Google+ circles happen onto this game, they may see a tiny image of your profile picture to indicate that you're one of the people they know who's played this game. For more info about exactly what information gets shared with whom, click the "Learn more" link in the box's lower-left corner. Before a Google+ game can share anything, it will show you all the ways it might share info about your playing activity, and you can usually limit which circles or people it shares that info with. So go ahead and click "Got it, let's play."

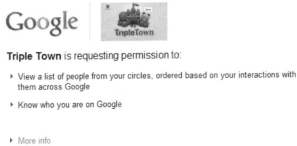

Now you get the details: A pop-up window appears with info about what the game wants to access. It may not be clear exactly what each item means; to learn more, click the tiny triangle to the left of each item.

Triple Town is requesting permission to:

▸ View a list of people from your circles, ordered based on your interactions with them across Google

▸ Know who you are on Google

▸ More info

Allow access　　No thanks

By proceeding, you agree to the application's Terms of Service and Privacy Policy

That's quite a bit more descriptive. Basically, Triple Town wants to see who's in your circles, order them by how you interact with them, and connect your profile to your game playing and progress. The game will know you're playing, and may share that with your friends if they stop by the Games section, but before it can actually create a post about your playing, you'll have a chance to choose which circles that post gets shared with. Still, if this all sounds like too much data-mining for you, click "No thanks" and move on to another game. Otherwise, click "Allow access," and the game will launch in your main browser window.

Google | Triple Town

Triple Town is requesting permission to:

▾ View a list of people from your circles, ordered based on your interactions with them across Google

   View a list of people from your circles that you may want to engage with
   The list is ordered based on your interactions with these people across Google
   View public profile information for these people

▾ Know who you are on Google

   Associate you with your public Google profile

▾ More info

✉ You can email the developer of this application at: spryfoxgames@gmail.com

[Allow access]   [No thanks]

Each game is different, but most have a few common elements. Most games include a button like the one in the lower-right corner of Triple Town that reads "Invite friends to play!" The incentive for the game makers is wider exposure, and perhaps some of those additional players will purchase in-game items, or pay for versions of the game that contain more levels and features. Triple Town, for example, lets players buy virtual coins with real money (yes, you read that right) so they can buy items that help them improve their scores, and feel all is right with the (virtual) world.

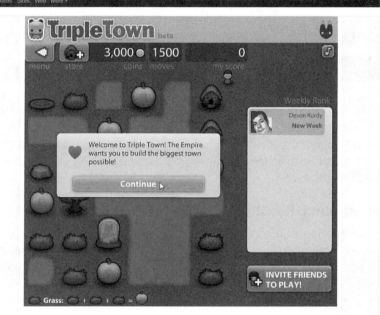

NOTE To purchase in-game items through Google+, you need a Google Checkout account. Google Checkout lets you pay for items online with a credit card, direct bank debit, or other means, through a secure, encrypted system tied to your Google account. Google+ will open a new web page to let you set up a Checkout account if you lack one, or you can set one up on your own, at any time, by heading to *www.google.com/checkout*.

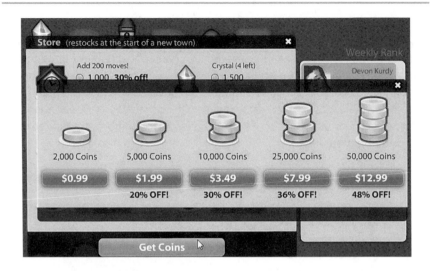

Another thing most Google+ games do is offer you a tutorial when you first arrive at the game window. Triple Town, for example, starts off simple, showing you how to place objects and making it clear that the goal is to line up three or more of the same thing (hence the name!). Some games let you watch a video that shows how to play.

Sharing Game Results

As you roll along in Triple Town (or your game of choice), you get tips about advanced features, pick up little hints about how to boost your score and achievements, and so on. Next thing you know, you might end up a little bit obsessed with this game. To spread your new obsession, you can share your score with your Google+ circles.

If you click "Share!" (or whatever similar button your game provides for brag-ging), you'll get a sharing box similar to the post-composing box, where you can add a comment, decide who to share with, and then click Share to pull the trig-ger or Cancel if you change your mind. If you've used Facebook for any length of time, you know that people who constantly share their game achievements and ask for help (with, say, their virtual farms) can quickly become annoying. Google+ tries to avoid this by making it easy to block game notifications (page 192), but still—make your game boasting and begging an occasional thing.

Some games in Google+ won't end up being worth your time, but others might be remarkably fun distractions that require nothing more than a web browser. And joining your friends—and competing against them—makes the games even more fun. Best of all, your scores and achievements are automatically saved and linked to your Google+ profile, so there's no need to worry that you'll lose hours of achievements by forgetting to save.

Joining a Game

IN SOME GAMES, INVITING your friends to play from within the game merely means suggesting that they play it, too, and then comparing scores. In other games, you can ask your Google+ contacts to join up with you, so that their playing benefits you, and vice versa. Games like CityVille and Crime City are good examples of this kind of networking game: When other people join Crime City because of your invite, they're added to your "mafia" and you get more power.

It's usually pretty obvious how to ask others to join a game—most games have "Invite friends to join" buttons in prominent places. Asking others to join a game works just like sharing a post, in that you choose the people or circles, preview the message, add your own comment if you'd like, and then send it out.

When someone receives your invitation and decides to join in, they'll arrive at the same screen you saw when starting the game, complete with reminders about privacy, data use, and sharing. When they're all the way into the game, they'll see how joining through your invitation has benefits for both of you.

Everything else in the game is the same for that player, although they might occasionally see your character while they're running around robbing mini-marts, planting turnips, or whatever. If you've invited them into a more direct competition, like a poker game, then you'll see them across the virtual table.

Take it from an author who knows his weaknesses—Google+ games can be really fun and pretty addictive, if you find the right one. Sharing your achievements and habits with friends is fun, too—as is being surprised by which of your no-nonsense friends is cranking their way through Bejeweled Blitz.

Index

Have it your way.

Google+

THE MISSING CD

There's no CD with this book; you just saved $5.00.

Instead, every single Web address, practice file, and piece of downloadable software mentioned in this book is available at *missingmanuals.com* (click the Missing CD icon). There you'll find a tidy list of links, organized by chapter.

Don't miss a thing!
Sign up for the free Missing Manual email announcement list at missingmanuals.com. We'll let you know when we release new titles, make free sample chapters available, and update the features and articles on the Missing Manual website.